- Sort

DECE

*Making a Difference in Education*

How can we get educators to use research evidence?
A review of the best ways to get evidence into use from many areas of public policy

by
Stephen Gorard,
Naomi Griffin, Beng Huat See and Nadia Siddiqui

Durham University Evidence Centre for Education
https://www.dur.ac.uk/dece/
@DECE_DU

# Summary

Over decades, there have been calls by concerned stakeholders to improve the quality of education research, and some progress has been made towards creating a more secure evidence base in some areas. However, there has been no equivalent improvement in secure knowledge about how best to get that evidence into use, or even what difference it makes when such evidence is used. This book looks at what little is already known about different ways to get research evidence into use in education. It does so by summarising the results of a large-scale review of the literature. A total of 323 most relevant studies were found across all areas of public policy, and judged for quality and contribution. Very few were of the appropriate design and quality needed to make robust causal claims about evidence-into-use, and even fewer of these concerned education. This means that despite over 20 years of modest improvement in research on what works in policy and practice, the evidence on how best to deploy such evidence is still very weak. The results of the review suggest that providing access to raw evidence or even slightly modified/simplified evidence is apparently not an effective way of getting it used, even if that evidence is presented to users by knowledge-brokers, in short courses or similar. The most promising approaches, for both policy and practice, involve selecting high quality evidence, engineering it into a more usable format, and presenting it actively or iteratively, often via a respectable conduit or through population measures such as legislation. Having the users actually do the research is also a promising approach in some areas. Research funders should support such approaches, help to build up libraries of successfully tested programmes, and stop expecting each individual study they fund to have impact. Publicly-funded users including policy-makers should be required to use evidence-led programmes from such libraries, where they exist and are appropriate and relevant to their aims. Researchers need to be scrupulous, looking at their new evidence in the context of what is already known and not seeking 'impact' from single-studies. More and better research is needed on the best routes for evidence-into-use. However, the improvements required of all parties are as much ethical in nature as they are technical or scientific.

# Acknowledgements

The work of this review was assisted by funding from the Faculty of Social Sciences and Health, Durham University, and by comments and suggestions from colleagues in the Durham University Evidence Centre for Education.

# List of contents

## List of tables

**Abbreviations used in the text**

DfE – Department for Education, the relevant government department for England

EEF – Education Endowment Foundation, near government organisation funded to generate evidence to reduce low attainment by disadvantaged students

ESRC – Economic and Social Research Council, the UK funding council for social science research

ESSA – Every Student Succeeds Act, a US bill that requires the use of evidence for higher levels of federal funding

MAT – Multi-Academy Trust, a kind organisation running many schools in England

NFER – National Foundation for Educational Research, a not-for-profit organisation conducting research

RCT – Randomised control trial, a robust design for testing the causal impact of interventions

REF – Research Excellence Framework, a mechanism for funding UK university research, based on its prior quality

SSIF – Strategic School Improvement Fund, a DfE funding mechanism to support school improvement based on evidence-informed approaches

# Chapter 1 – The problems of getting evidence in use

*Research quality and impact*

Evidence derived from research is considered important in contributing to improvements in policy and practice, as agreed by most professionals working in public policy and practice (Lohr et al. 1998, Davies 1999, Head 2015). High quality evidence can reportedly lead to important gains for individuals, the public, and society (Palmer 1999, Simpson 2003). For example, the UK Department for International Development has been involved in evidence-led intervention programmes in developing countries, leading to a 22% reduction in new-born mortality through assisting with breast-feeding in Ghana, and a 43% reduction in deaths for HIV positive children through enhanced antibiotic use (Alliance for Useful Evidence and Cabinet Office 2017). Often evidence does not improve policy/practice directly but instead saves a considerable amount of money from being wasted on ineffective approaches, and so permits more effective use of limited time or funding (CAHO 2008). Knowing what does not work is therefore very valuable and too often ignored or downplayed.

In consequence, there have been increasing demands over 20 years from funders and governments for publicly-funded research in education policy and practice to be of higher quality and to have real-world "impact" (Hillage et al. 1998, NRC 1999, Mosteller and Boruch 2002, Smith 2003). In other areas of policy the same demands have come from academics themselves (MacIntyre et al. 2001). This increasing emphasis on generating more robust evidence of "What Works" in the UK is exemplified by some of the work funded by the Economic and Social Research Council (ESRC) Teaching and Learning Research Programme, ESRC Evidence Network, ESRC National Centre for Research Methods, ESRC Quantitative Methods Initiative, Nuffield Foundation Q-Step programme, and perhaps most notably for education by the Education Endowment Foundation (EEF) in England. These and other initiatives follow or shadow similar ones in the US such as the Institute of Education Sciences, while other countries have since produced their own versions of many of these initiatives.

The situation in terms of research quality now is far from perfect, and commentators are still claiming that most education researchers are not doing replicable 'scientific' work (Hazell 2019). Many of the relevant initiatives have taken wrong turns, or even been 'captured' by those acting to return to the prior situation in which complex analyses were preferred to powerful research designs with simple answers comprehensible to a wide audience, for example. There have also been unwarranted attacks on these initiatives by others with vested interests in the status quo, as has also happened in relation to improving evidence in other fields (Rosenstock and Lee 2002). Nevertheless, all of these initiatives *have* helped to improve the quality and range of research, and therefore the understanding of effective interventions to inform education policy and practice. A growth in experimental designs, coupled with natural experiments, better and more open official data, and data archiving, have all encouraged improvements in robust evaluations of proposed programmes, in education as elsewhere (Rutter 2012).

The situation in terms of the use of this improved research evidence in policy/practice is less clear. Even in fields like health services, evidence has long played only a minor role in practice (Palmer 2000). Helping embed secure research findings into policy and practice has been a concern for at least as long as the concern about generating improved primary evidence itself (Lawrence 1990), and is this concern worldwide (Koh et al. 2010). The importance of using evidence to improve effective public services crosses both national and policy boundaries (van de Goor et al. 2017). It should now be an integral phase in the overall research process (Gorard et al. 2017), and a review of evidence uptake in health, justice, traffic policy, and drug policy did find work on the improved use of evidence in all of these areas (Oliver et al. 2014). Their review did not cover education specifically.

The UK ESRC want "Knowledge Exchange and Impact" embedded at the heart of all ESRC research, and they present awards to studies regarded as having outstanding impact. This engagement and impact is monitored via the website Research Fish long after the projects they funded are complete. The UK Research Excellence Framework (REF) for funding research in universities requires the submission of academic impact case studies, which are then assessed by panels as being of one of five levels of quality. Other funders and stakeholders similarly, and quite naturally, not only want high quality evidence to be generated but also want that robust evidence to be of use for real-life.

*The three problems*

Unfortunately, this apparent desire by all parties for research to have a greater role, via 'impact', has generated at least three problems. First, it is not at all clear that the research that has the greatest impact is actually of the highest quality. For example, the REF impact case studies must be based on research judged by the relevant panel of reviewers to be of at least 2* quality. This rating is from a scale of 0 (not really research of any value at all) to 4* (world-leading). In REF2014 around 30% of all work was judged to be 4*, and 76% overall was judged to be 3* (internationally excellent) or better. It is therefore astonishing that work considered to be among the lowest 24% in quality should be celebrated as having had any impact in real-life. In no way does this match the expressed ambition of having robust evidence-informed policy and practice. It would make more sense for impact cases studies to be based only on research graded as 4* (i.e the best available). Similarly, studies have been given ESRC awards (prizes) for the quality of their impact simply because their results are in widespread use, even where the evidence does not warrant such impact, or in some cases where the impact actually contradicts the findings of the research itself. It is as though merely claiming to make a difference is considered 'impact' of the kind that is needed, whether it is evidence-led in reality or not.

For example, one of the pieces of social science work with the greatest impact in the UK over the past 20 years has been the social mobility study by Blanden et al. (2005). Their report claimed that social mobility in Britain was worse than in many other countries, including

Scandinavia, and that it was getting worse over time. All three main political parties made these 'facts' the basis for their 2010 elections manifestos, a mobility tsar was created, followed by a cross-party Social Mobility Commission, and billions of pounds of taxpayers funding was and still is being allocated to solve the problem. However, the original report was clearly in error. Their book presents and compares the data for the 1958 and 1970 British birth cohorts in order to claim there is a difference over time (with the 1970 data suggesting worse social mobility than for 1958). The data for Norway are from 1958 with father's income for parents, and son's income for children. This is exactly the same format as for the 1958 data for Britain. And this 1958 British data shows income mobility about the same as Norway and other Scandinavian countries. Yet Blanden et al. (2005) used the worse British figures for mobility in 1970 to compare with the 1958 data from Norway, despite the 1970 figures being in a different format, and based on average parental income (and having further differences as well). And despite publishing the more comparable 1958 figure in the *same paper* they used the less comparable 1970 figures in order to make the claim that the situation is worse in Britain. This kind of elementary mistake should be obvious to anyone reading their paper.

All of this means that high quality research may be used inefficiently, weak and erroneous research may have unwarranted impact, and researchers may be tempted to push for unwarranted impact, and to over-claim the impact that their work has had. It is extremely difficult to demonstrate whether any research has truly had any beneficial impact (Noyes and Adkins 2016). For evidence to be shown to have been used or cited in use is not enough. We need better and more secure ways to measure its impact (Lavis et al. 2003). But this is not easy, because as well as being used instrumentally, which is its most obvious role, evidence can play a conceptual or even a symbolic role in practice, and so still claim to have influence (Davies 2012). Policy-makers also report using evidence to identify the problems needing solutions or to encourage political action, as well as to generate policy alternatives (Apollonio and Bero 2017), and for planning and justification of action rather than evaluation decisions (Dobbins et al. 2001).

There is clear evidence that many researchers do distort and exaggerate their impact claims, feeling under pressure to do so by their funders' emphasis on impact, and through a desire to do well in REF assessments or similar (Chubb and Watermeyer 2017). Instead stakeholders and funders should insist that only high quality evidence should have impact, and that it only counts as impact if what is done by users is in strict accordance with that evidence. Of course, users will not simply read evidence and then act in some kind of automatic way. Evidence-led use only means that the users' actions must be in *accord* with the evidence. This may mean that they do nothing, the evidence may modify what they do slightly, or it may completely transform an educational process. However, the ESRC giving an impact award to a study that showed that an educational intervention did not work, but was still widely used, and being promoted by the researchers, is quite wrong. This illustrates the scale of the first problem (the greatest impact is not coming from the best research), and that it affects even stakeholders who apparently want evidence to have real-life impact.

The second major problem is that the idea of single studies having any impact at all may be misconceived. There is little direct replication of studies in education. Nevertheless, when conducting a systematic review or similar it is clear that there are many studies reporting on any one issue, and that both the quality and the substantive findings of these studies differ. It is important to focus on, or give more weight to, the most robust and trustworthy evidence (Gorard 2013). But it is also important to realise that a best evidence summary may contain contrary findings. A single study may be of high quality but contradicted by a larger number of equally good studies. In this case, the 'best bet' is to base policy or practice on the overall picture from all good studies, using the contradictory study as a caution (because it may still be the correct result). One study should probably not have much, if any, impact by itself, except as a caution against any intemperate action that goes against its findings. Awarding grades and prizes for the impact of specific pieces of research is therefore actually contrary to the very idea of evidence-informed education, and should cease. We also need considerable improvement in judging and agreeing what high quality research is for any context, and what the aggregated results of an entire field are. Both of these issues are discussed further in this book.

The third major problem is that progress in generating good evidence for real-life use has not been matched by an equivalent growth in knowledge about how such evidence is best handled in order to have appropriate impact, even in areas like health (Moore et al. 2011, Powell et al. 2017). In paediatrics, 20 years ago, practice guidelines were seldom based on the findings from randomised control trials or similar, and the evidence of the benefits of using such guidelines was non-existent (Bergman 1999). The former has improved considerably, the latter has not. Similarly, it is still unclear across most areas of public policy which interventions are effective in boosting influence at a policy and practice level in real-life (Ellis et al. 2005, Langer et al. 2016). As McLean et al. (2018, p.44) point out in health science "It is paradoxical that funders' efforts to get evidence into practice are not themselves evidence based". Corrigan et al. (2001) suggest that "we need to adopt an evidence-based approach to evaluating the dissemination of evidence-based treatments".

Any claim that research has had impact is a clear causal one, and so ought to be evaluated to the same standard as the initial research itself. The DfE in England (Coldwell et al. 2017), EEF (2018), and the US Coalition for Evidence-based Policy, among others, have been seriously considering how to translate and implement research findings. However, at the moment, recommendations for the implementation of evidence are not themselves based on good evidence from evaluations of how to implement evidence. To show that research has had an impact on policy or practice outcomes, we need first to determine that research has indeed been used, and how. But even in areas like public health, there is little rigorous work measuring the outcomes of translational or implementation research, or knowledge translation, in policy/practice environments (Davis et al. 2003, Zardo and Collie 2015).

In evidence-based medicine, Simons et al. (2018) explain that while training in the use of evidence might increase the knowledge of practitioners, although the evidence for this is weak, there is almost no evidence that this leads to changes in actual behaviour, and no evidence at all that it improves patient outcomes. There is perhaps even less evidence on how to get evidence into use in education (Wentworth et al. 2017). The situation has not changed much over 20 years (Smith 2000). For teachers, Jones (2018) asks:

> Where is the evidence that evidence-based practice has a measurable impact on learning and outcomes? In other words, which schools can point to exam results and say they have improved because of evidence-informed practice? In other words, where is the backing for the claim that schools and teachers should use evidence – and particularly research evidence – to inform practice? As otherwise, all we have is the assertion that the use of evidence is a good thing.

In combination, these three problems for evidence-into-use can lead to wasted opportunities, and even harm for the education system. They are additional to any practical difficulties in getting practitioners and policy-makers to use evidence for the benefit of their work at all (Epstein 2017). Most education reforms worldwide are still not evaluated in any coherent way, for example (Whitty 2016). Such monitoring in situ should be expected, and funded, as part of the normal cycle of research. Further, in those cases where academic research has been used to formulate practical interventions, there is often no follow-up evaluation or routine monitoring to ensure its effectiveness in real-world applications. As a society, we need to use the best evidence available in the most effective way possible.

This is a practical and conceptual issue with implications beyond education, and an ethical concern for the majority of the population who both fund education via their taxes and charity-giving, and use its services for themselves or their families. Large amounts of public money are still being spent around the world on education initiatives that have no basis in evidence, little chance of working, and are continued even when their ineffectiveness has been revealed, creating the possibility of harm (Carrier 2017). There is always a kind of opportunity cost, given that every unwarranted policy uses time, effort and resources that could have been used for a genuine improvement. All of education is damaged when persuasive but poor quality evidence has widespread influence, as happens routinely in the UK, with programmes like Brain Gym or Learning Styles being used in classrooms, universities and training programmes. Developments in how to gauge and agree on the trustworthiness of evidence are therefore also essential.

The suggestion is that despite decades of work to enhance policy/practice through the use of evidence, many ministers, civil servants, and practitioners, still see research and use as disconnected, and an area of considerable weakness (Perry et al. 2010, Rutter 2012).

These three problems, especially the third, are the focus of this book, which reviews the evidence on how best to get good evidence into use. The book summarises the methods we used, and how we judge the quality of research, and then looks at the existing evidence on the different approaches to getting research evidence into use, the range of factors which influence the uptake of high quality research evidence in policy or practice, how these have been evaluated so far, and which are the most effective pathways for evidence-into-use in particular contexts.

Although the most effective routes for evidence-into-use might vary between policy and practice, and some would argue that evidence use in policy is very different to practice (Black 2001, Lassnigg 2012), others have found similarities between the two (Rickinson et al. 2017). Both are covered in this book. Policy and practice uses of evidence are probably each more varied within themselves than between the two, and the two are anyway inextricably linked. School and classroom evidence-based changes can influence larger policy, and policy can make the use of effective strategies more feasible at school and classroom level (Slavin 2017). As a comparison, debates about how best to manage TB patients in sanitaria in the early 1900s onwards involved practical issues of training, qualifications of staff, facilities needed, isolation, and scale. These practice issues were then all made irrelevant by a very different kind of research that simply cured TB through drugs and vaccinations. High and low level interventions are connected, and not always in a predictable way. This is one reason why both are dealt with together here.

*A word about the terms used*

The terms evidence-based, evidence-informed and evidence-led are all in widespread use. They all suggest a desire by policy-makers and others to consider relevant and high-quality evidence systematically, and to avoid erroneous or biased uses of evidence, perhaps for political ends (Parkhurst 2017). No commentators are suggesting that evidence should be the sole basis for action. Professional knowledge and experience, values, and other factors will all play a role (Greenhalgh and Wieringa 2011), as will public opinion (Burstein 2003). Some commentators draw a distinction between evidence-based referring to a programme that facilitates the application of evidence without practitioners' involvement in the decision making process (Melnyk 2007), and evidence-informed referring to practice that enhances the application of evidence with users' involvement in the decision making process (Abbott et al. 2013). Some studies refer to translation and others to knowledge adoption (Brown 2012a). This book prefers the term "evidence-led" to encompass all such ideas, and instead draws distinctions between types of programmes (such as population or individual measures), and types of outcomes (changes in knowledge/attitudes, in behaviour/practice, and in educational or other results for members of the wider public).

"Use" in this book refers to the implementation of research evidence in real-life settings, and to the ways in which behaviour, policies, and practices can be guided by research evidence. The focus is on social science evidence use, in and from education, as widely conceived, and in other fields of public policy. It excludes the use of evidence by academics in their own research.

"Evidence" is taken to be the result of deliberate research. It is the available body of information used to indicate whether a social science claim is trustworthy, and dependable enough to be used in non-academic settings in a way that will affect peoples' lives or use public resources.

## Chapter 2 – The methods used in our review

The research question addressed in this book is:

> What is the existing evidence on the most effective routes for getting high quality evidence into use for (education) policy and practice?

This was addressed via a review, looking also for evidence from wider public policy for lessons that could be useful in education. Priority was given to robust evaluations of getting evidence into use, but the number of such studies was limited. Much of the more robust work found turned out to be in health and related fields. The review also picked up previous systematic reviews, secondary data analyses, economic appraisal methods, implementation evidence and in-depth views from stakeholders and public consultations. These are all incorporated or cited as appropriate.

*Identifying the studies*

The studies were identified through the following means:

- Systematically searching electronic databases (below) and Google Scholar
- Searching journals, bibliographies and websites
- Following up citations in reports and reviews found in the searches
- Adding literature already known to the reviewers from previous work in the field
- Proactively contacting key stakeholders via email

The bulk of the materials came from a search of the main educational, psychological and medical databases. The search was as designed to be as inclusive as possible to identify a wide range of both published and unpublished literature, such as dissertations/theses.

*Electronic searches and databases*

We searched using EBSCOhost database, which covers British Educational Index (BEI), PsycINFO, ERIC, Applied Social Sciences Index and Abstracts (ASSIA) OpenDissertations, Education Abstracts, Education Administration Abstracts, PsycARTICLES. We also conducted searches of JSTOR, Web of Science databases and EBook selection through First Search. Our experience suggested that there may be relevant literature on the use of evidence in policy in practice in medicine and similar fields. For this reason, we also searched Ovid Medline and PubMed databases. To be more comprehensive and to ensure that our materials were up-to-date, we also used the Google Scholar search engine.

Having identified the databases, we developed the search strings. These were first tested on the EBSCOhost database for sensitivity. Following several iterations we found that individual search terms combined with syntax either found very little, or else included evidence on the primary research that was intended to be used (i.e. almost everything). This is because of the double use of terms like 'evidence' in searching for evidence on evidence-into-use. We found that the more successful search terms included the terms or synonyms of the terms in the following combination of statements:

- Use of research in policy/practice
- Impact of using research evidence in policy/practice
- Most effective way of getting policymakers/practitioners to use evidence

The search was intentionally broad and inclusive (with no geographical, disciplinary or date limiters) since the strategy or approach of getting evidence into practice and policy cuts across all disciplines. For example, successful approaches in medicine and economics might be applied to education. There are useful lessons that can be learnt from these other disciplines.

The number of records identified from each of the databases is as shown in Table 2.1.

Table 2.1 – Number of research reports found in each database

| Database | Number of hits |
|---|---|
| Ebscohost | 31,291 |
| Web of Science | 1,717 |
| Ovid MEDLINE | 107 |
| EBook selection through First Search | 6,856 |
| Jstor | 263,242 |
| Google Scholar | 3,050,000 |
| Total | 3,353,213 |

The search was conducted separately for each of the search phrases twice, once for policy and once for practice. However, there was a lot of overlap between policy and practice, and so we aggregated the results here. Given the broad and open search, we set the search to present us with the most relevant ones first. Because of the number of records found, we made a decision to stop reviewing titles when the next five pages or 100 results (depending on which came first) after the last relevant articles were found revealed no more relevant items. This means, of course, that we may have missed some important reports, but we are confident that this review is both the biggest ever done in this area, and unlikely to have transformed conclusions through discovery of a few more studies.

*Screening*

Initial screening of titles and abstracts in order of relevance (see above) created a set of 582 distinct reports that were broadly about how to use evidence in real-life applications, based on a quick scan of titles and abstracts. Further screening removed 262 pieces as duplicates or substantive duplicates leaving only 320. Of these 22 were subsequently excluded as not relevant on reading the full piece, and further 25 were found in the citations of previous systematic reviews. The final number of all pieces retained in the review is 323. A large number of these are conceptual or small-scale descriptive studies with no clear research design, and most of these are only cited briefly in the review that follows.

*Inclusion criteria*

- Any literature (published and unpublished) that is about ways of helping policymakers/practitioners to use evidence
- Literature in any fields that is about getting research evidence into policy/practice
- Reports with any date and country of origin

*Exclusion criteria*

- Studies that are clearly not about research
- Studies that are not about use of research evidence in policy or practice
- Studies not available in English

Even though the search was broad and wide, the topic of evidence use is so generic that there will be relevant studies, perhaps even high quality ones, not picked up in searches. This review therefore cannot be definitive, but it represents the biggest and most comprehensive to date.

*Data extraction*

Descriptive and conceptual studies were useful as background references and were cited where relevant but were not data extracted. The more promising, empirical studies were data extracted, based on the full texts. This involved creating a brief description of the paper, the study design, sample, methods of data collection and data analysis and the reported outcomes. Each was then assessed for trustworthiness using the procedure in the next section.

*Synthesising high quality evidence*

It is crucial that only the most robust research evidence has any impact in real-life (Gorard et al. 2017). It could be, and probably already has been, disastrous for the education of individuals where incorrect or misleading evidence has had enhanced use in real-life (Parkhurst 2017). This is something that needs widespread agreement by all parties, and is in many ways a precursor to all else here. One step towards agreement would be a standard process for judging how trustworthy any body of research is. The following generic procedure has been suggested to help assess the security of the findings from any study, when synthesising the evidence on any topic (Gorard 2018). It has been reported as easy to use, and leads to consistent judgements between raters.

The quality of each research report and therefore the trustworthiness of its findings are judged based on the underlying research design, scale, missing data, quality and relevance of measurements, fidelity and validity. The ensuing five possible (but essentially arbitrary) levels of quality are summarised in Table 2.2. Each study can be given a rating representing its lowest row description for any of the first five columns. The first step is to identify the information on each of these issues from the report of the research being assessed. If the report does not include important information, or is written in such a way that the reader has no way of understanding it, then the research must be rated as having no security, and is not to be trusted.

Many studies do not have a clear design, and this is a weakness. If the research question is about changes over time then a longitudinal or trend design is required. If the research question compares outcomes for two or more groups then the answer should involve a comparative design. If the research question is causal then a stronger design such as a randomised control trial (RCT) or regression discontinuity should be deployed.

Table 2.2 – A 'sieve' to assist in the estimation of trustworthiness of any research study

| Design | Scale | Missing data | Measurement quality | Threats | Rating |
|---|---|---|---|---|---|
| Strong design for research question | Large number of cases (per comparison group) | Minimal attrition, or non-response | Standardised, pre-specified, independent, valid | No evidence of diffusion, demand, or imbalance | 4 |
| Good design for research question | Medium number of cases (per comparison group) | Some attrition, or non-response | Less valid but valid in context | Little evidence of diffusion, demand or imbalance | 3 |
| Weak design for research question | Small number of cases (per comparison group) | Moderate attrition, or non-response | Issues of validity or appropriateness | Evidence of diffusion, demand or imbalance | 2 |
| Very weak design for research question | Very small number of cases (per comparison group) | High attrition, or non-response | Poor reliability, too many outcomes, weak measures | Strong indication of diffusion, demand or imbalance | 1 |
| No consideration of design | A trivial scale, or scale is unclear | Missing data huge, or not reported | Not reported, or unclear | So many threats as to be useless | 0 |

Whatever the design, a large study is more believable than a small one, given that all other factors are the same. This is true whatever the methods of data collection and analysis (the need for rigour, when research is used to influence real-life, cannot be evaded by citing a "paradigm", for example). The strength of any study in terms of scale rests largely on the size of the smallest group in any comparison or statement of findings. Perhaps the biggest problem with the reporting of most research is lack of clarity about missing data – such as refusal, non-response, dropout, or error. All missing data from a planned study is a source of possible bias in the results, because there will be a reason why the data is missing (it must not be assumed to be random). And data can be missing at many levels, and for many reasons. All missing data reduces the trustworthiness of evidence, and the greater the missing data the worse the study is.

The "measurements" or observations used to represent research outcomes needs to be reliable in the sense of being capable of being judged to be the same by different observers. They must also be valid and isomorphic representations of what they are intended to measure

(Gorard 2006). It is important that any outcome(s) of interest is specified and made clear before any study is conducted, if at all possible. This is to prevent researchers or users subsequently dredging a larger number of variables for those that show some kind of 'success', 'failure' or other pattern.

There are a large number of further issues that could enhance or reduce the trustworthiness of research results. All are judged in the same way, in terms of how they might reinforce or reduce trust in the research findings.

This sieve approach was part of the development of the EEF padlock security rating, which has a similar purpose (while being more technical and involving less judgement). The EPPI Centre (for systematic reviews) has developed a "Weight of Evidence" framework, and there are other alternatives with the same intended purpose in fields other than education. Only research that is graded highly by one of these appropriate methods ought to have direct impact in real-life.

The sieve approach suggested here underlies the judgements made in the rest of this book about the quality of existing research on evidence-into-use. In a later section of the book, evaluations of how best to get evidence into use that are rated as 1, 2, 3 or 4 via this method are cited in bold. These all have at least some kind of counterfactual (or similar), and are summarised in Tables 6.1 to 6.4 (Chapter 6). All other citations can be assumed to be of a lower quality of evidence for the purposes of the research question posed in this book, and are descriptive or speculative, or they may be high quality for another purpose but do not address the key question of how best to get evidence-into-use.

# Chapter 3 - The quality of research on evidence-into-use

As will be seen, very little work on evidence-into-use has been found in our search that is anywhere near the level of quality and rigour that is currently required by users and funders when producing the evidence to be used in policy or practice in the first place. Despite all of the progress that has been made over 20 years in improving research in education and beyond, almost none of this progress is reflected in the evidence on evidence-use (Murthy et al. (2012). Only a small number of studies found in this review have any kind of counterfactual to illustrate what would have happened if the approach (to evidence-into-use) suggested had not been used. A review by Moore et al. (2011) similarly found little good evidence about which strategies increase the use of evidence in population health policy and programmes. Another review by Oliver et al. (2014), covering a range of policy areas, found little empirical evidence on the implementation of evidence in policy more generally. More useful studies were reported in a review by

LaRocca et al. (2012), and these are dealt with as individual reports in the substantive review in this book.

This new review found some examples of researchers describing (or claiming) the impact of their own research (Husen 1987, Cambridge Public Policy 2017, Sen 2017). There are some reasonable evaluations of professional development in education, but these were only marginally about the use of evidence (Powell et al. 2010). There is a range of work in most fields of policy and practice, including thought pieces on how evidence-use might work or be improved[1], or developing conceptual models for improving the uptake of evidence[2]. Much of this is in nursing and health sciences, and for specific

---

[1] Humes and Bryce 2001, McCluskey and Cusick 2002, Rubenstein and Pugh 2006, Glasgow and Emmons 2007, Zlotnik 2007, Green 2008, Graham and Tetroe 2009, Schmittdiel et al. 2010, Brown 2012b, Lingard 2013, Brown 2014, Lawton and Rudd 2014, Blase et al. 2015, Bowen and Zwi 2005, Jordan and Cooper 2016, Parkhurst 2017, Peterson 2018

[2] Kitson et al. 1998, Moulding et al. 1999, Rycroft-Malone et al. 2002, Nutley et al. 2003, Swinburn et al. 2005, Aarons et al. 2011, Mitton et al. 2007, Feldstein and Glasgow 2008, Kitson et al. 2008, Wandersman et al. 2008, Tapp and Dulin 2010, Chaudoir et al. 2013, Lubienski et al. 2014, Mackie et al. 2015, Dimmock 2016, Witting 2017, Farley-Ripple et al. 2018, Graham et al. 2018, Ritter et al. 2018

diseases or conditions, and there are so many competing models and theories that syntheses have been done involving dozens of them (Sussman et al. 2006, Tabak et al. 2012). Some looks at the competences needed for knowledge transfer (Mallidou et al. 2017). Some of this descriptive work is quite esoteric given that so little has been done on the basic effectiveness of any of these ideas (McCormack et al. 2002), and much of it is repetitive over many years (Harvey et al. 2002). There are existing models and ideas which theorise some aspects of evidence-into-use in different fields (Mendel et al. 2008, Damschroder et al. 2009, Ward et al. 2009a, Dingfelder and Mandell 2011, Nilsen 2015). There are also toolkits and similar guidelines for evidence translation, or using evidence in policy-making (Ademokun et al. 2016), and ideas for training practitioners in evidence use (Melnyk et al. 2008, Winters and Echeverri 2012). There is a book on implementing research findings in education with one chapter on how evaluations of implementation might take place, but findings from robust evaluations (Rosenfield and Berninger 2009).

None of these ideas have been tested properly, and so none provide robust evidence of their effectiveness. The existing evidence on the relative 'effectiveness' of approaches is largely limited to personal experience, case studies, observational data, interviews and surveys, in passive designs[3]. There are even systematic reviews of such interview-based work (Innvær et al. 2002). There is a very large body of research that has asked those involved in evidence-use how it works and what the barriers and facilitators are[4], and some of this work is summarised later in this book. There is work that has looked for traces of evidence in policy documents (Gollust et al. 2014, Castellani et al. 2016). There are small before-and-after studies (Hammond and

---

[3] Grol 2001, Fineout-Overholt et al. 2004, Macaulay and Nutting 2006, Nutley et al. 2007, Baumbusch et al. 2008, Jewell and Bero 2008, Daugherty 2008, Friese and Bogenschneider 2009, Jack et al. 2010, El-Jardali et al. 2012, Mady 2013, Cacari-Stone et al. 2014, El-Jardali 2014, Daly et al. 2014, Lawton 2014, Ongolo-Zogo et al. 2014, Sirat and Azman 2014, Gross et al. 2015, Naude et al. 2015, Shroff et al. 2015, Connelly et al. 2016, Ellen et al. 2016a, 2016b, Langer et al. 2016, Imani-Nasab et al. 2017, Marquez et al. 2018

[4] Garner et al. 1998, Haynes and Haines 1998, Grol and Wensing 2004, Harper 2004, Brehaut and Juzwishin 2005, Fink et al. 2005, Mold and Peterson 2005, Cameron et al. 2011, Honig and Coburn 2008, Brown et al. 2009, Wilson et al. 2009, Nelson et al. 2009, Elliott and Popay 2000, Orem et al. 2012, Urwick 2014, Thomas et al. 2015, Kirigia et al. 2016, Boydell et al. 2017, Ellen et al. 2018, Tricco et al. 2018

Klompenhouwer 2005, French et al. 2012), and relatively large scale surveys (Chaloupka and Johnston 2007). But there is almost nothing testing out these ideas in a robust manner in any field, and even less in the fields of education policy and practice.

Other previous work has tended to be conducted over a very short time, and at a very small-scale (Strambler and McKown 2013, Brown and Rogers 2015, Admiraal et al. 2016), even though change based on existing users adopting new ideas from up-to-date evidence often takes a long time to appear in more objective measures (Gardner et al. 2008). For example, a US study that randomised districts to a reform model based on tried and tested programmes found little or no difference in student state test results after only two years (Slavin et al. 2013). However, there *were* more indications of positive effects for reading and maths by the fourth year.

What is needed in order to address the research question for this book are robust evaluations of evidence into use, over a longer period, using a variety of routes and approaches. Some prior work has been done in this area, but the routes to, and mechanisms for, evidence use have rarely if ever been robustly evaluated (Langer et al. 2016). It is quite shocking how much research is reported about how to get evidence into use, but how little of it is really of any use for the purposes of this review.

# Chapter 4 - Descriptive findings on the barriers to evidence use

The book looks first at some of the primarily descriptive research found in the rapid review, so this section is largely based on the conceptual and in-depth work about barriers and facilitators for getting evidence into use, as outlined in the previous section. The stronger evidence based on more robust designs appears in the next substantive section of the book.

*Primary research quality*

A major barrier to coherent evidence use in real-life is the antagonistic stance of many researchers to the very idea that practical or scientific knowledge is possible in education (Biesta 2010, Lancaster 2016). This may be a particular problem in education (Hemsley-Brown and Sharp 2003). There are criticisms of what counts as 'evidence', and suggestions that social reality is so complex and irreducibly rich that useful evidence of 'what works' is not even possible (Marston and Watts 2003). If true, then evidence-informed attempts at improvement simply would not work, or may even be detrimental. For example, in a correlational study based on 5,238 children in the Early Childhood Longitudinal Study-Kindergarten Cohort data (1998-1999) in the US, it seemed that reform-oriented instruction produced slightly worse results in maths than traditional pedagogy (characterised by textbooks, teacher-directed, chalkboard and routine practice and drill). And highly qualified but less experienced teachers were most likely to use the non-traditional methods, and they produced the worst results (Park 2013). Similarly, a number of educational interventions validated by the What Works Clearinghouse have reportedly been found to be ineffective when rolled out into practice. And this has led to some commentators concluding that using research evidence to improve education will always mislead rather than inform users, or even that 'effective' evidence-based practices and policies should never be implemented (Pogrow 2017), or even that evidence-led education is just not possible (Cain 2015). However, such conclusions are illusory and based on cherry-picking of evidence – the very thing that evidence-informed approaches would decry as misleading. They are also created partly by the lack of research on the implementation of innovations in real-life

(Gorard 2013). Much primary research has been in efficacy style, and much less has concerned the rollout of interventions (Glasgow et al. 2003).

Such objections to the use of robust evaluations in social science are based on misunderstandings (Bell and Peck 2016), although of course designs like RCTs can be used poorly, just as with any other research design. Even where an intervention has been *robustly* evaluated and found to be successful on many occasions in the past, it still may not 'work' when rolled out into practice or on all occasions or in all contexts. It is easy to find examples where a programme thought to be effective did not lead to improvement when used by others. This is to be expected in any scientific endeavour. Such programmes are not proven; they are only examples what has worked in the past. Similarly, it is possible to find examples of interventions that have no firm basis in research evidence but could improve outcomes (Vujcich et al. 2016). This happens perhaps through luck, or individual teacher prowess in education, or other factors acting in parallel with the intervention. No approach has ever been absolutely proven to work or not to work. None of these points would be an argument for not using the approach that has the best chance of success. The judgement on which approach to use can only ever be based on the 'best bet', informed by the best evidence available at the time.

A more appropriate concern is the lack of attention to unintended consequences from attempts to improve education (Zhao 2017). In medical research, it is more usual to investigate the 'side effects' of any treatment, but evidence-based education research has so far seemed to be relentless in pursuit only of what works. Side effects are effects, and need to be examined as much as any other outcomes. Unintended consequences can be beneficial, making any successful intervention even more attractive, or they can be harmful. In either case they need to be considered in any cost-benefit analysis. For example, an effectiveness trial of improving writing found some small benefits, but at a cost of worse progress in other subjects (EEF 2018).

Actually the biggest barrier preventing the widespread generation and use of high-quality evidence is probably the lack of research competence among researchers themselves whose job it is to provide evidence in education – and as exemplified *in extremis* by those who write off evidence as completely useless. Much of the research evidence used in practice, even in the What Works tradition, is untrustworthy (See 2017). There is still too little good quality research for use in policy (Schilling et al. 2009, Alliance for Useful Evidence 2014). Because the quality of evidence in many areas is so low, this allows policy-makers either to ignore evidence or pick supposed 'experts' who can support their ideology (Cook and Ludwig 2006). More generally, this leads to poor access to good quality relevant research for users (Oliver et al. 2014).

Key stakeholders such as policy-makers, practitioner bodies, and senior researchers tend to agree reasonably well both that (UK) education research is not good enough for real-life impact and why this is so. According to them (in Taylor and Gorard 2002), the issues were:

- shortage of 'quantitative' skills – both to use such skills and to 'consume' research that employs quantitative tools or methods;
- propensity for non-cumulative, small-scale and/or 'flawed' research;

- limited attention paid to causal links and the effectiveness of teaching and learning artefacts;
- concerns over the lack of rigour and lack of innovation in 'qualitative' research
- constraints created by the friction between 'qualitative' and 'quantitative' 'methodological identities'.

These problems may be exacerbated by:

- limited or missing research 'apprenticeships' for many educational researchers;
- particular demands of education departments to train teachers at the expense of educational research;
- lack of continued professional development throughout the typical educational researcher's career.

However, again this picture may be at least partly illusory. Even at that time, the self-reports of a large number of researchers, and UK-wide submissions to the RAE (an earlier version of REF), suggested no shortage of so-called 'quantitative' skills or large-scale work

(Gorard et al. 2004). Following the initiatives outlined at the start of this book, the situation will be, if anything, even better in this regard. The absurd idea of 'methodological identities' does still persist, and much publicly-funded research is still of poor quality (Gorard and Siddiqui 2018a). But this poor quality of work applies to 'quantitative' and multiple method work, of the kind required supposedly by the What Works approach, as much as it does to anything else (Gorard et al. 2017). In fact, this kind of work may be more misleading because it tends to be taken more seriously by users than the more common small-scale, uninventive and sloppy journalistic, solely 'qualitative' work (which still forms the majority of UK education research).

A more commonly cited area of weakness for researchers is their ability to communicate their findings to users (Rutter 2012). In some accounts at least, education researchers have traditionally played little part in helping others to use their evidence to improve the education system (Miller 1999). The process of knowledge transfer needs more capacity-building work – perhaps especially in universities (Cooper et al. 2009, Perry et al. 2010). In order to influence policy, policy 'entrepreneurs' may need to be political fixers, networkers, and good storytellers (Alliance for Useful Evidence and Cabinet Office 2017). Universities or other research organisations may need to spend more on research translation, media and communication, and provide suitable incentives for academics to conduct the different kinds of public-facing work involved, and to create appropriate outputs for users. To some extent, this kind of improvement is already underway.

*Skills and attitudes of the users*

Despite claims that they do (Bogenschneider et al. 2013), overall neither policy-makers nor practitioners in education actually use much external research evidence (Galway and Sheppard 2015). There is a gap between how much teachers say they value research evidence, and what they do in practice (Procter 2013). They also have a different and wider definition of "evidence" than academics and researchers (Alliance for Useful Evidence 2014). Teachers tend to look for and use research for quick help for immediate concerns such as preparing a lesson (Drill et al. 2012), but they do not seek research evidence very often (Mahoney 2013). They tend to trust the evidence appearing in peer-reviewed journals but also find this the hardest evidence to access (preferring word of mouth summaries).

As with the producers of research, the attitudes and skills of users of research can be a major barrier to enhanced use of evidence. Users are rarely scientists themselves, or otherwise competent to judge the quality of research (Alliance for Useful Evidence and Cabinet Office 2017). Policy-makers in health are not generally able to judge the trustworthiness of research, or tell the difference between a review and a systematic review of evidence (Brennan et al. 2016). And this is despite the confidence of their managers (for civil servants and medical administrators) that all of their staff had the necessary skills. Even when users are suitably trained and can make good judgements about the quality and relevance of evidence for use in public policy issues in abstract examples, they are much worse at doing so when considering a specific real policy issue. In the latter context they tend to give greater weight to anecdotes and personal experiences (Crocco et al. 2017).

Policy-makers and practitioners in education may say that they want and use good evidence (Penuel et al. 2017). And governments often start out at least espousing the use of evidence, but seem to become less interested and more dogmatic the longer they are in power (Perry et al. 2010). Policy is generally not designed or rolled out in a way that permits robust evaluation of its benefits (Rutter 2012). Policy-makers often select only a subset of the available evidence, especially where the research was conducted or paid for by their department, in order to help validate their political judgement. This is a process nicknamed 'policy-based evidence making'.

Similar issues arise with practitioners. Those in medical practice, for example, have cognitive biases just like everyone else (Epstein 2017). They may ignore an evidence-based route in order to respond to a patient's emotional needs, be influenced by a specific traumatic episode, or over-treat a patient out of concern (Grol and Grimshaw 2003). They may use evidence in some areas of their work and not others (Corcoran 2003). Educators can often be sceptical about evidence, or treat it in a superficial way (Finnigan et al. 2013). Some teachers and education policy-makers simply deny the value of using evidence at all. Some, perhaps less honestly, espouse the use of evidence but are not actually led by it in reality – continuing with approaches or interventions for which there is no evidence, or even when they are aware that there is solid evidence against (Gorard 2018).

The attitudes of users may be a particular problem in education, where so many people behave as 'experts' (Hemsley-Brown and Sharp 2003). Education is reputedly one of the most value-laden areas of public policy (ATL 2013). So, even if research is of high quality it will make no difference unless potential users are receptive to new knowledge (Brownson 2017). Often, attitudes and behaviour must be changed at an individual, team, organisation *and* system level in order for a new evidence-informed approach to take hold (Harvey and Kitson 2015). Influencing a ministerial decision in the UK usually involves lining up the Minister, special advisors, analysts and civil servants to agree, and to put forward the same proposal.

School leaders appear content to plan school improvement without referring to robust evidence (Graves and Moore 2018). Some school leads are already explicitly stating that they will ignore evidence in their schools, with a backlash against evidence-informed approaches, the use of RCTs and the feeling of being told what to do in what they see as their own domains (Cain 2019). Fraser et al. (2018) suggest that school principals do state that they value evidence when it is reported formally in articles and similar, but in practice they tend to rely on local informants and other educators when deciding which educational programmes are most useful to them. Real improvement might depend primarily on users having a desire to use evidence-informed approaches, and being shown the benefits of doing so more clearly.

In public health, a survey of policy decision-making suggested that research evidence was the least commonly used source of information, with internal reports being the most common (Zardo and Collie 2015). Policy-makers' most trusted sources include governments, advocates, lobbyists, and industry figures (Dodson et al. 2015). All also policy tends to be influenced by political pressures, public opinion, stakeholder bodies and pressure groups, and perceived practicality (Cooper et al. 2009, Thomas et al. 2015, Jackson et al, 2018), often in a way that is quite unjustified by programme performance (Head 2015. Dick et al. 2016). Choices for education practitioners tend to be based more on history, tradition and convenience than evidence.

In order to use evidence to inform policy, policy-makers would need a range of skills and knowledge that they may not currently possess – such as the ability to to source, evaluate and use evidence (Oliver et al. 2014, Jackson et al. 2018). David Laws, a former Minister of Education in England, claims that education policy-makers are not very good at dealing with evidence, their civil servants are not very good at providing them with secure evidence, and many policies rely largely on 'hunches' (The Guardian 2017). Civil servants generally have a culture that does not value the rigorous use of impartial evidence

(Rutter 2012). Policy-makers, as with all individuals, may be tempted to ignore evidence unfavourable to their chosen ideas. Cowen (2019) suggests that the situation is worse than this. Policy-makers help define what sort of evidence counts as robust, and this makes evidence-based approaches such as trials of classroom programmes attractive. Any blame attaches to teachers for using (e.g. learning styles) or not using (e.g. phonics) programmes led by evidence. The work of the EEF in England, for example, is largely silent on the structural features of the national education system. So it cannot pass judgement on or criticise things that policy-makers are largely responsible for, and where these same policy-makers routinely ignore or resist evidence – such as when suggesting the expansion of grammar schools (Gorard and Siddiqui 2018b).

For both policy and practice a major barrier is the time and effort needed to keep up with the necessarily changing evidence on any topic (Gerrish and Clayton 2004). The organisations that actually deliver education such as schools need more capacity to find, share, understand, and use research. Otherwise, even the best research will have little impact (Cooper et al. 2009). The University of Bristol (2017) found that teachers reported lack of time as the biggest barrier to engaging with evidence, but perhaps the biggest barrier for practice in education is that teachers are largely unaware of the availability of evidence (Sparks 2018).

In healthcare, even when new evidence clearly shows that a current treatment is ineffective or harmful, it often takes ten or more years for a new approach to be adopted. Sometimes change has to wait for practitioners to retire or die, and be replaced by newer ones with more up-to-date knowledge (Epstein 2017).

In the US the Education Commission of the States produced a primer for policy-makers on how to source suitable research, read it critically, and use it appropriately (Royal Society/British Academy 2018). This has been widely used. Something similar could be tried for other settings such as the UK, and for other parties such as practitioners. One important step would be to make lawmakers state explicitly what any new policy is intended to achieve, so that success and failure can be evaluated properly (Hess and Little 2015). This probably involves changing the ways in which policy is made, so that policy-makers routinely assess the available evidence, ensure that it is embodied in their decisions, and continue to do this as new evidence comes to light (Sisk 1993). They must not be dogmatic. Above all, policy-makers and practitioners must want to use evidence, and to understand why doing so is both practically and ethically important, and wider public must demand this as well. This is an ethical issue more than a technical one.


*Other possible barriers to evidence use*


Other barriers include the lack of timeliness in the research process, and the multiplicity of other demands on users. Although most education research can be deemed relevant to a real-world issue by its producers, evidence is often still not seen as relevant by users, especially policy-makers, because it is not timely enough. UK funding mechanisms for research such as the REF and ESRC have the major advantage that they are largely independent of government, and so permit considerable academic freedom. However, ESRC funding can take up to one year to obtain, and REF funding occurs only every seven years or so. And academics have other priorities as well. This all means that other non-academic bodies have been set up to deliver quicker research findings to funders like the EEF, but can then come to rely on their funding support. This can lead to mutual dependency of a kind that is an enemy of evidence-led improvement (Gorard et al. 2017).

Policy-makers value timely evidence relevant to specific time-limited policy issues (Thomas et al. 2015), and any mismatch in the timelines of the users and producers of research simply means that evidence is likely to be ignored (Rutter 2012). This is a common occurrence because ministers and even administrations generally have a short life-span, much shorter than the period needed for the proper implementation of education reform (Perry et al. 2010). There is also considerable mobility within the UK civil service. A former UK minister of education has complained that civil servants rarely have enough knowledge to provide up-to-date evidence (The Guardian 2017).

At present and for as long as evidence has been available, public policy is seldom based on solid evidence, and is largely the product of other influences and issues (Jackson-Elmoore 2005). These include the need for quick solutions or for secrecy, political promises and expediency (Alliance for Useful Evidence and Cabinet Office 2017), personalities, personal relationships, available funding, convenience, heavy marketing by vested interests (Hess and Little 2015, Slavin 2017), self-interest (Noyes and Adkins 2016), and ideology (Rutter 2012). Based on UK Prime Ministers' memoirs, Perry et al. (2010) suggest that politicians rely more on their instincts than evidence, distrusting much of the education establishment, preferring to listen to a trusted few, or to their favourite think tanks. Based on local authorities' engagement with evidence in London, Al Hallami and Brown (2014) suggest that how evidence is treated varies according to the ideology of the majority political party in the authority.

The power of the media has also increased, often forcing politicians' hands in a direction contrary to the evidence.

However, media attention is not a simple route (a silver bullet) for researchers to influence policy-makers (Zimmerman 2004). And even newer forms of feedback to governments, such as social media, may be biasing policy-making away from more robust evidence. There is also considerable scope for urban myths and serendipity to influence outcomes.

Some practitioners can feel constrained in acting in accordance with evidence because they lack the authority to change existing practice (Gerrish and Clayton 2004). And building the capacity of policy-makers and others to use evidence can be regularly hindered by rapid staff turnover, and changes in administration (Waqa et al. 2013).

How can all of these barriers be best overcome, and how strong is the evidence on how to achieve this?

## Chapter 5 - Review of evaluations of evidence-into-use

This section looks at the actual effectiveness of different kinds of routes to impact, in education and beyond, as far as the existing limited evidence permits. There is a wide range of possible routes for getting evidence-into-use, and these could be classified in a number of ways. Raw evidence from research can simply be accessed by research users, as when policy-makers and their advisers are given access to research reports and articles. This is a cheap form of knowledge transfer, but it requires a skilful user to search, read, and summarise the evidence, and then to implement the changes. Alternatively, the raw evidence can be engineered into an artefact, or redrafted to another format, for easier use. But this may do injustice to the fuller evidence, and it makes the evidence harder for users to judge in terms of its underlying trustworthiness compared to similar artefacts, that may not be as scrupulously evidence-based.

Table 5.1 – Two dimensions of evidence-into-use

| | Passive transfer | Engagement in transfer | (inter)Active transfer |
|---|---|---|---|
| Plain evidence | a) e.g. open access to journals | b) e.g. journal clubs | c) e.g. practitioner inquiry |
| Modified evidence | d) e.g. EEF Toolkit for practitioners | e) e.g. Think tanks | f) e.g. internships, research schools |
| Engineered evidence | g) e.g. lesson plans | h) e.g. hotlines, helpdesks | i) e.g. legislation for population measures |

Whether research findings are used as they are, or used to create an artefact that is meant to be easier for policy/practice, there can also be variation in how much activity goes into the attempted transfer of knowledge, by the researcher or developer. Modified research findings can be simply made publicly available, as with the increasingly popular Toolkit approach, or there can be active engagement in explaining what the results are and why they should be trusted. The former is what the National Institutes of Health (NIH) refers to as dissemination or "the targeted distribution of information and intervention materials to a specific public health or clinical practice audience", while the latter is about implementation, or "the use of strategies to adopt and integrate evidence-based health interventions and change practice patterns within specific settings" (Gonzales et al. 2012).

There will be many other factors than the two mentioned above (level of modification and level of activity in transfer), but considering these two as different dimensions, the situation can be summarised as in Table 5.1. These nine cells or variants form one of the ways in which the existing evidence is classified in this review. The evidence relevant to each cell is discussed in turn.

*Cell a – plain evidence, passive transfer*

The idea that evidence is created by experts and then drawn on as necessary by policy-makers and practitioners is not an accurate description of the process of evidence-informed evidence use (Gorard 2018). It is not even a useful prescription for what should happen (Nutley et al. 2002). Policy processes are generally so complex that simply giving research users access to information about research (as in cell a in Table 5.1), and expecting them to act upon it, is unlikely to be effective (Honig et al. 2017, Coutts and Orlik, 2017). There is not likely to be a direct and unadulterated impact of research on policy (Noyes and Adkins 2016), and anyway evidence is often adapted by users during its operationalisation (Cohen et al. 2008). Even in relation to practice, the passive dissemination of research evidence is not seen as effective (Grol and Grimshaw 1999).

In social work and welfare, there is evidence from author surveys and bibliometric data that Campbell Collaboration standard systematic reviews of evidence are regularly downloaded, and cited by other writers

(Brandy et al. 2018, Maynard and Dell 2018). The Campbell review authors themselves claimed that their reviews had been used to make changes in policy or practice, but whether this is really so is difficult to assess. Such claims are not in themselves of great value as evidence of impact. Some commentators even believe that such reviews are far from the best way forward in summarising research, preferring to look instead at the programme theory (Pawson 2006), or arguing against meta-analyses (a specific form of synthesis of evidence) as pseudo-arithmetic (Simpson 2017). Systematic syntheses of evidence do have problems (Wolgemuth et al. 2017), and may anyway have little impact in practice, without further translation and activity (Haines et al. 2004, Green et al. 2016).

In a review of evidence from 18 systematic reviews of evidence-into-use in health practice, **Bero et al. (1998)** confirmed that the passive dissemination of such research evidence is largely ineffective. Of course, access can be improved by changes to infrastructure and IT, but policy-makers still say they would prefer active presentations such as skills workshops (Hawkes et al. 2016). However, see below.

*Cell b – plain evidence, engagement in transfer*

Users of evidence for policy and practice are rarely trained specifically to handle plain evidence presented passively (Connell and Klem 2000). As foreshadowed when discussing barriers (above), it is clear that policy-makers at all levels from elected representatives to civil servants, when asked, report that training in the use of evidence helps them to make sense of it or prepare their own evidence briefs (Pappaioanou et al. 2003, Uneke et al. 2012, Uneke et al. 2015a, Uneke et al. 2015b). Training may not be enough. Their capacity to use evidence might be improved through tailored workshops and extensive mentoring (Haynes et al. 2018). Policy-makers also need to have research skills, and this needs to be part of their job descriptions (Peirson et al. 2012). Despite this, training and dissemination workshops often have poor attendance after a fanfare start, especially for the most senior policy-makers (Dagenais et al. 2013). However, policy-makers also report preferring having research mentors or knowledge brokers on standby (Rolle et al. 2011, Traynor et al. 2014). Committees for sharing policy evidence did not work well, as not supported by management (Hoeijmakers et al. 2013). One promising but so far not evaluated way forward is the use of software to help users to commission their own systematic reviews (Campbell et al. 2011).

Generally, research on policy-makers' and practitioners' uptake is based on self-reports. There is little robust causal evidence on the types of intervention that actually encourage users (in health or anywhere else) to take account of systematic reviews in their decision making. Simply sharing research articles made no difference to schools' policy and practice in 11 districts in Canada (Levin et al. 2011).

One review, that also covered some RCTs reported separately in this book, suggested that a more active approach was needed (Perrier et al. 2011). A study by **Taylor et al. (2004)** compared a convenience sample of 145 health practitioners allocated to a half-day critical appraisal skills training workshop (73), or a wait list (72).

The knowledge and ability to appraise the evidence in a systematic review were higher in the workshop group, but there was no difference in the attitude towards using evidence, and no evidence of subsequent changes in practice or behaviour. Providing three interactive workshops on finding and using evidence from a reproductive health library led to more knowledge and use of the library, but made no difference to or improvements in practice, according to the review by **Gülmezoglu et al. (2007)**. Similarly, a trial involving an educational visit to help obstetricians and midwives select and use evidence from a Cochrane database found no difference in resultant practice between 12 obstetric units in the intervention group and 13 in the control **(Wyatt et al. 1998)**.

So although users say they prefer these more active approaches, they are actually no better than simply making evidence available, in terms of changing behaviour. Overall, there is little reason to think that access to plain evidence will assist widespread use, even when there is some engagement such as training for users.

*Cell c – plain evidence, active transfer*

Teaching staff in England are reported as being less confident about engaging in research themselves, than in reading the research of others (Hammersley-Fletcher et al. 2015). Nevertheless, it has been argued that schools working alongside researchers would sharpen knowledge of what evidence means and how it can strengthen the work of schools.

**See et al. (2016)** evaluated an intervention in which a cluster of nine partnership primary schools agreed to look at a research journal article on enhanced classroom feedback, hold a series of cascading training events for all staff, and then conduct three action research cycles in just over one school year. The intention was to improve pupil attainment. Some teachers found it very hard to understand the primary evidence they had read, and often implemented the findings in an inappropriate way. The academic outcomes and progress scores for pupils overall were no better than for five comparison schools in the local authority, and for all maintained schools nationally. Even such interactive transfer of primary evidence (cell c in Table 5.1) is therefore challenging for users. Similarly, Levin et al. (2011) found little difference from study groups or even school districts conducting research themselves in the take-up of evidence in schools' policy and practice in 11 districts in Canada. Teachers need clearer guidance, professional development, and modelling of effective strategies on the use of research evidence, to improve attainment. There needs to be some more engineered 'conduit' to translate research evidence into practical guidance for teachers – which could be in the form of lesson plans or protocols.

In health, staff in units that were involved in producing research reports or reviews were more likely to understand them. But they were no more likely to use the results than staff in units not involved in the research (Kothari et al. 2005).

Sometimes, however, impact *can* be achieved by the potential users participating in research themselves (the ultimate interaction with research evidence), and not just accessing the evidence. For example, nurse-led research is gaining some attention as a critical pathway to practical and effective ways of improving patient outcomes

(Dufault et al. 1995, Curtis et al. 2017). Similarly, McLaughlin et al. (2000) reported that involving teachers and school administrators in research teams meant that the research was more targeted at their concerns, and the staff learnt more about research use, and were more likely to support use of the findings. Similar claims (and they really are only claims) have been made based on participatory research on aging (McWilliam 1997). In a small RCT run by **Tranmer et al. (2002)**, 28 nurses, who worked in two clinical research groups on developing their own research protocol (18 high participation, 10 low participation), reported more use of research evidence in practice, than a comparator group of 207 nurses. An even higher gain was reported for the group that also discussed and critiqued the research literature among themselves.

A powerful equivalent in education could be randomised trials (i.e. not action research) set up and run by teachers themselves (Churches 2016). Both Siddiqui et al. (2015) and Gorard et al. (2016a) reported trials led by a set of unrelated schools, and then aggregated by the authors. Both trials were moderately successful. They showed that volunteer teachers were able to run robust evaluations with limited external guidance, and each intervention had a positive impact on student outcomes (effect sizes of around 0.25). The studies suggest that this approach to getting evidence into use by involving teachers in research is feasible. But they had no proper counterfactual for the evidence-into-use aspect – and provide no indication that the two popular interventions would not have been used by these schools anyway even in the absence of the trial.

Overall, the evidence on cell c is inconclusive.

*Cell d – modified evidence, passive transfer*

A number of commentators/studies suggest that research evidence is more likely to be used if its findings are simple or simplifiable (Noyes and Adkins 2016), or adapted to context (Bertram et al. 2018), perhaps as summaries, overviews or policy briefs (Chambers et al. 2011). Simpler and more defined descriptions or protocols of interventions appear to have a better likelihood of success (Langer et al. 2016). Or at least, presentations of the evidence need to be in user-friendly formats that help policy-makers in their decision-making (Pew Charitable Trusts 2014). **Rosenbaum et al. (2010)** found in two small trials (with only 15 cases in the smallest group) that providing a clear summary of findings can improve understanding and retrieval of evidence from a systematic review. However, this was part of an interactive workshop, and there is no evidence on whether practice changed as a result afterwards.

In the Toolkit approach, an inventory of approaches or programmes is created, and categorised in terms of the evidence for their effectiveness, cost and benefits. These are often then simply made available or publicised for users (rather than it being made impossible to use programmes that are not supported by robust evidence). This passive approach does lead to some engagement, as evidenced by downloads and similar metrics, so the idea is relatively popular. In fact, a version of the EEF Toolkit is now being developed in many countries (Collins 2018). But there is little or no evidence that Toolkits then influence practice, and none at all so far that they lead to improved attainment. There are claims that converting research into a more journalistic format authored by the researchers themselves, such as via the Conversation, increases engagement and so impact (Zardo et al. 2018).

However, it is not clear that simply modifying research findings into easier formats (cell d in Table 5.1) leads to any better results, with a passive approach to transfer, according to the summary of systematic reviews (see above) by **Bero et al. (1998)**. See also Siddiqi et al. (2005) discussed below. In health care, merely disseminating best practice guidelines is insufficient to alter practice in most cases (Miller et al. 2006, Gonzales et al. 2012). **Seers et al. (2004)** looked at the use of an evidence-based algorithm for use by hospital wards when delivering oral analgesics. This led to no difference in observed practice on the four wards involved (two in the intervention group, and two comparators).

In three small trials (334 cases overall), **Buljan et al. (2017)** compared a scientific abstract, a plain language summary, and an infographic, as ways of presenting knowledge about the results of Cochrane systematic reviews in health. The audience included doctors (111 intervention, 60 control), university students (46 intervention, 18 control), and lay consumers (45 intervention, 54 control). All three groups preferred the infographic (or the summary if not given the infographic), and rated it better than the other formats for reading and user friendliness (effect sizes of around 0.5). However, the infographic was no better for actually imparting knowledge of the findings of the review. The format of delivery of evidence does not always seem to matter much. **Di Noia et al. (2003)** compared offering health guidance materials for 188 professionals via pamphlets (55 cases), CD-ROM (64) or the internet (69). The CD-ROM and the internet were linked to greater improvements in self-efficacy and reported behavioural intentions, but the study did not provide actual changes in treatment as an outcome. In one Campbell review of 24 studies (including 20 RCTs), e-learning compared to no learning was effective in improving evidence-based health care knowledge and skills, but made no difference to attitudes and, most crucially, no difference to clinical behaviour, and was silent on patient outcomes *(Rohwer et al. 2017). Across six trials (from eight studies in a review) of using summaries of evidence for decision-making, evidence summaries were deemed* easier to understand than complete systematic reviews, but their ability to increase the use of systematic review evidence in policymaking was inconclusive (**Petkovic et al. 2010**). *Therefore, just presenting modified summaries of evidence to users*, and expecting them to act upon it is very unlikely to work as a method of translation to use (Alliance for Useful Evidence and Cabinet Office 2017).

A systematic review of methods of teaching new medical trainees about evidence-based medicine found nine RCTs and compared a number of modes of delivery (Ilic and Maloney 2014). These included lecture versus on-line delivery, lecture versus small group work, directed or self-directed, and different groupings by disciplines. All were linked to increases in knowledge, but there was no difference between them. Another study compared the results of systematic reviews in health to policy-makers as factual briefs or in the form of stories. The results were mixed (Brownson et al. 2011).

The initial and continuing development of practitioners such as teachers is an obvious area where robust evidence relevant to practice can be included (but currently is not in the UK). There is no evidence concerning how effective this approach would be.

The Literacy Octopus trials evaluated the impact of providing teachers in a total of 13,323 schools with research summaries and evidence-based resources to improve teaching, with or without light touch support (**NFER 2017**). After two years, there was little or no increase in any of six measures of teachers' use of research, and no improvement in pupils' Key Stage 2 English scores compared with the control group. Simply disseminating research summaries and evidence-based resources to schools does not so far seem to be an effective way for research organisations to support schools in improving pupil outcomes. This is an important study both in terms of its scale, and because it is one of only a few that assessed the impact of trying to improve research uptake on student outcomes. Schools may need more help than this in transforming such materials into beneficial change in the classroom.

*Cell e – modified evidence, engagement in transfer*

What if the modified evidence is presented more accurately?

Pederson et al. (2015) examined the procedures for giving evidence to parliamentary committees in the UK, Denmark and Netherlands. They found that only a small group of 'actors' generally volunteers to be involved, and this affects the concentration and type of evidence presented, and so handled by committees. Invitations tend to garner fewer responses than open calls, but from a wider range of participants.

A relatively common suggestion as a way forward is greater collaboration between researchers and policymakers (van de Arend 2016). This could be based on 'learning communities' for policy (or practice). Academics and researchers must welcome officials and others into such communities, to discuss new evidence as it emerges, and how to incorporate it in their planning (Brown 2014). The Alliance for Useful Evidence and Cabinet Office (2017) give an example using research from six Asian and African countries. The Future Health Systems consortium worked on a set of key strategies for improving the uptake of evidence into policy, such as improving the technical capacity of policy-makers, better packaging of research findings, the use of social networks and the establishment of fora to assist in linking evidence with policy outcomes. There are many other examples of such communities of practice (Langlois et al. 2016).

Such relatively formal consortia are one example of a kind of conduit between research itself and its users. Others might include knowledge brokers (Dobbins et al. 2009a, Ward et al. 2009b, 2009c), think tanks, What Works Centres or clearing houses, and some charities. Such intermediaries may have an important function in translating research findings into more acceptable formats, and connecting researchers to potential users (Cooper et al. 2009, Edwards 2010). However, **Dobbins et al. (2009b)** found that having a knowledge broker of this kind had no clear impact on research use compared to tailored messaging and simple access to a registry of research. Their study was based on 108 health departments in Canada (72 randomised to intervention).

Advocacy organisations can also pursue an agenda that is not clearly related to the overall evidence, taking a partial view but using their political and media expertise to influence policy outcomes (Malin and Lubienski 2015).

Evidence can be presented in summary form to users by expert commentators as it is at international conferences such as ResearchEd. However, previous work in health found no good evidence that educational outreach interventions were effective in changing the behaviour of practitioners (**Siddiqi et al. 2005**). In that systematic review, the authors found 44 studies that met their selection criteria, but many had weak designs, and the overall evidence was inconclusive on outreach, use of mass media, and reminders. One-off workshops are not generally effective (Miller et al. 2006), nor are mailings or short courses according to a review of 55 studies in the existing literature (**Davis and Taylor-Vaisey 1997**). No difference was found between the use of seminars and roundtables in encouraging the use of systematic review results in health policy (Dwan et al. 2015).

From a review including five RCTs and three interrupted time series analyses, **Murthy et al. (2012)** suggested that mass mailing a printed bulletin with evidence from systematic reviews about obstetric care may improve evidence-based practice. However this could only be for one key message, about a change that is simple to affect, and where the users are at least partly receptive already. Under other circumstances, or where more complex changes are demanded, this approach shows no promise.

One of the approaches that schools have adopted to assist the use of evidence has been to identify research leads or champions, whose role is to engage with the evidence in any area and then relay this in more digestible form to the rest of the school. Teachers report several challenges to this model, particularly staff turnover among research champions (Rose et al. 2017). There is a weak positive correlation between the level of engagement of teachers with research, and the attainment of their pupils. However, the relationship may well not be causal, or if it is causal then it may be inverse, perhaps because good teachers are anyway more likely to engage with research.

Recent pilot evaluations funded by the EEF in England, involving five self-selected schools, found little evidence that providing research evidence for teachers in this way makes any difference to their student attainment, at least in the short term (**Griggs et al. 2016**). The intervention was based on a designated research champion covering five schools (and 2,075 pupils), auditing schools' needs, and providing a variety of generic and targeted development activities. Providing research evidence in this way may not increase teachers' reported use of research. Similarly, **Speight et al. (2016)** found no evidence of impact on future teacher behaviour (only some changes in attitudes) from encouraging teachers in 10 self-selected primary schools (teaching 280 pupils) to use modified or summarised research evidence on issues such as metacognition. The intervention involved a learning community network (cell e in Table 5.1). Both pilot evaluations suggested that such interventions need considerable support from school leaders (not just research leads).

The **University of Bristol (2017)** evaluated the use of workshops or Research Learning Communities, in which experts discussed research evidence with evidence champions from schools. There was some indication that this led to more interest in research among teachers, bu there was no overall improvement in reading results for 5,462 pupils in 119 schools (60 intervention, 59 randomised to control). It may, of course, take longer than two years of involvement for any impact to be seen. This study is important because it is one of only three found in this review that is a direct test of a method of implementing evidence on learner outcomes.

Professional development is seen as more effective when school leaders also participate (Alton-Lee 2011). Leadership in creating a framework in which evidence use is encouraged and made easier is considered important in a number of fields (Newhouse 2007, Hauck et al. 2013).

An RCT involving the directors of 126 zoos (63 randomised to each group) concerning education about sun-screening suggests that tailoring dissemination materials with follow-up phone calls leads to no advantage over simply making generic material available

(**Lewis et al. 2005**). A synthesis of evidence from two studies of promoting evidence-informed decisions in nursing (tertiary care), within a review of 30 studies, found that engagement in the form of educational meetings and having an evidence mentor made no difference to nurse engagement in evidence-led behaviours (**Yost et al. 2015**). **Abdullah et al. (2014)** reviewed 10 studies of mentoring and individual attention from more senior colleagues in health as aids getting knowledge of evidence into use, but nine of these studies were multi-faceted with mentoring as only one component, making it impossible to draw a clear conclusion about the impact of mentoring. The remaining study suggested some improvements in nurse practitioner behaviour in relation to evidence, but said nothing about the impact for patients. An earlier similar review by **Thompson et al. (2007)** found relevant studies to be of low quality in general. The four studies synthesised were inconclusive overall. Two found that researcher-led educational meetings with nurse practitioners made no difference to evidence uptake. Two were deemed effective, but had additional components, such as a local opinion leader running the meeting.

There is no evidence yet that just linking users and researchers in research projects, perhaps via user groups as encouraged by ESRC and others, is effective (McLean et al. 2018). There is also a danger that the intermediaries are subject to the same pressures as users (as described in the previous section), and so may distort or cherry-pick evidence to suit their user clients. It is not always clear whether think tanks, based on an ideology, are using evidence accurately or not (Reid 2016). Conduits must be firm, honest, independent and credible to all parties (Rutter 2012). They may include private consultancies (Sin 2008), although there is no evidence that this works either. The conduit groups must have access both to new research and to internal government documents (Williams 2010). In policy, the World Health Organisation recommendations for mother and child nutrition may provide a good example of evidence presented both fairly and usefully (Benmarhnia et al. 2017).

Several commentators commend the idea of the National Institute for Health and Care Excellence (NICE) for healthcare in the UK, and suggest an equivalent for other areas (Langer et al. 2016), including for education policy (Perry et al. 2010). A combination of such an evidence conduit and a learning community for education research has been proposed by the Royal Society/British Academy (2018) in the UK, and provisionally named the "Office for Educational Research".

Overall the evidence on engagement and plain evidence is inconclusive.

*Cell f – modified evidence, active transfer*

There are interventions for getting evidence-into-use in the health sector that have been tested successfully using experimental approaches, and which are potentially replicable in an education setting. Individual coaching on evidence-informed approaches in specific areas, with individual feedback, is perhaps the most promising approach (Miller et al. 2006), although an evaluation of a dental hygiene intervention based in 20 cities, with 385 registered hygienists randomised to intervention and 366 to control, suggests that self-study can be almost as effective and, of course, cheaper to implement (**Gordon et al. 2005**). Some "training" interventions based on small group workshops and follow ups have shown that knowledge among health practitioners increased at post-test, but there are no differences in treatment behaviour or patients outcomes according to a trial of 148 medical practitioners, with 73 randomised to intervention (**Forsetlund et al. 2003**). Similarly using communities of practice with software follow up was linked via a RCT of 37 mental health practitioners (18 in intervention) to having greater knowledge of a mental health intervention, but not to reporting greater readiness to change practice, or reporting actual change (**Barwick et al. 2009**).

Interactive multi-component interventions can improve therapists' and practitioners knowledge of evidence (**Davis and Taylor-Vaisey 1997**), and they can then change their practice behaviour (but not their attitudes), compared to passive dissemination of evidence according to a review of 12 interventions by **Menon et al (2009)**. The Translation Research in a Dental Setting (TRiaDS) project set out to improve evidence-based practices among Scottish dentists using behaviour-change theoretical models from the psychological literature (Clarkson et al. 2010). This led to a large cluster RCT involving 2,566 dental practices (1,999 intervention and 567 control), which demonstrated that an audit and feedback intervention was effective at persuading dentists to undertake anti-biotic prescribing in line with the current evidence (**Elouafkaoui et al. 2016**). There is further evidence from a systematic review of health care interventions that audit and feedback is the most effective way to get evidence into use, at least for the short term and often combined with other approaches (**Siddiqi et al. 2005**), although some studies find the combination only moderately effective (**Davis and Taylor-Vaisey 1997**). In fact, there may be generally more evidence of effective approaches involving feedback, reminders and education for professionals such as dentists, rather than policy-makers or the public (Haines et al, 2004). However, an older RCT providing feedback and advice to 36 medical residents (18 per group) on ordering expensive tests for patients was inconclusive in terms of reduction of inappropriate testing for the treatment group (**Ruangkanchanasetr 1993**).

Two way secondments between government and research departments are feasible, and are being increasingly attempted. It is an approach that has potential but, like so many others, has not been tested directly, and only considered via surveys and similar (Uneke et al. 2018). Research-practice partnerships have been appearing in the US, but again have not been evaluated properly yet (Coburn et al. 2013).

In summary, this is perhaps the most promising cell so far in terms of positive outcomes from more robust studies. The lessons are discussed in the next section of the book.

*Cell g – engineered evidence, passive transfer*

Successful UK REF case studies suggest that the under-pinning research having any real-life impact is usually invisible to teachers, and instead is embedded in artefacts such as services and technologies (Cain and Allan 2017). These can either change attitudes or are simply used on trust, such as in pre-prepared lesson plans and resources (cell g in Table 5.1). If transfer is to be passive then the intervention has to be so heavily engineered that its evidence-base is no longer clear to the user. An example would be clinical guidelines for nurses (Thomson et al. 2000). Teachers may object to being made to follow heavily engineered evidence in this way. Where school chains like MATs specify not only the curriculum and teaching style but also provide a script, teachers describe feeling like robots (Roberts 2018). Of course, it is not at all clear in this example that the scripts in question are robustly evidence-based, but the same reaction would probably appear even if they were. Although there are no good studies on this, it could presumably be an effective way of getting evidence into use. The evidence used must be high quality, and it must be translated faithfully into appropriate educational artefacts.

*Cell h – engineered evidence, engagement in transfer*

Some results for behavioural science (nudging) suggest that breaking an intervention down into smaller steps can be effective (Castleman 2015). As a result, it has been claimed in the US that school choice information is simpler and more visually digestible for parents, the architecture of school cafeterias subtly encourages children to select healthier eating options, and well-designed nudges can help students and families make active and informed decisions about the educational pathways they pursue (cell h in Table 5.1).

Some work on nudging has also been done on vaccine uptake in simulated conditions (Korn et al. 2018). **Dobbins et al. (2009b)**, in the same study described above, found that tailored, targeted messages to health professionals were slightly superior in encouraging evidence use, compared to merely providing access to research, or using a knowledge broker. Similarly, reminders were found to be among the most effective methods in a review by **Davis and Taylor-Vaisey (1977)**. In policy-making, it may be more effective to promote short-term steps, such as improving the ease and quality of bike-sharing schemes in cities, than to promote the same schemes with longer-term objectives, such as reducing air pollution (Li and Kamargianni 2018).

*Cell i – engineered evidence, active transfer*

Milne et al. (2014) describe software that provides policy-makers (in the field of child policy) with the opportunity to simulate the impact of research-led policies. However, this promising idea has not been yet been robustly evaluated.

The US Department of Education Investing in Innovation (i3) programme provided large grants for applicants wanting to improve attainment at their schools (https://www.ed.gov/open/plan/investing-innovation-i3). The largest grants required applicants to use only interventions rated as effective by the What Works Clearing House, from a short-list that had been robustly evaluated with success (Pogrow 2017). The US Every Student Succeeds Act replaced the No Child Left Behind Act. Under ESSA, to be eligible for school improvement funding, schools must use one of the top 3 categories of programmes – based on evidence-based interventions (California Department of Education n.d.). Oddly, the equivalent scheme in England, the SSIF (Gov.UK 2017) gave schools large sums of money for improvement but had no requirement that the most promising approaches, based on scientific evidence, should be used. In fact, the Public Accounts Committee (2015) stated that the Department for Education (DfE) in England:

> does not do enough to make sure... good practice is adopted in weaker schools... To date, the Department has supported schools to use the Pupil Premium [extra funding for schools taking poorer pupils] effectively primarily by funding the Education Endowment Foundation to carry out research into the evidence base for what works. However, it has done less to incentivise schools to use best practice and only recommends, rather than mandating, Pupil Premium Reviews for schools that do not use funding well. This is particularly worrying given concerns expressed to us that schools that perform poorly are less likely to seek out advice for themselves... As the evidence base grows, the Department should develop the necessary mechanisms to make *sure* schools use effective interventions with disadvantaged pupils.

A similar idea to compulsory use of Toolkits is also possible for policy-makers, and has been tried in Mississippi (Arinder 2016). All requests for new programmes would have to be screened for their supporting evidence including long-term cost-benefit. This could be the key role for legislative bodies, deciding on programmes not in terms of ideology but public interest.

Kansagra and Farley (2012) draw a distinction between evidence-based interventions in health that are implemented at an individual level - like the prescription of metformin for those diagnosed with diabetes, which is a treatment that requires initial and continuing actions by the patient - and those implemented at a 'population' level – such as the fluoridation of water to prevent dental caries. The latter have a lower cost per individual treated, and are more reliable than individual treatments. Another example might be using evidence from health science to plan urban spaces better to encourage health-enhancing exercise to reduce the incidence of chronic diseases (Giles-Corti et al. 2015). Or the imposition by international finance of, reportedly, evidence-based solutions on the government of developing countries (Williams 2016). An example from nursing might be the requirement for all clinical practice policies and procedures to be evidence-based (Oman et al. 2008). Such an approach has been enforced in health settings via the use of report cards (Valentine et al. 2104). It is likely that if evidence is to improve education successfully then more of such population-level measures need to be developed, validated, implemented and evaluated (cell i in Table 5.1).

However, even these very promising approaches have not been clearly evaluated (Longjohn 2012). A further caution might be that legislation or other structures enforcing the use of a specific evidence-based approach could discourage critical evaluation by practitioners (Sisk 1993). The ideal would be evidence-led professional judgement by users of all kinds, including Prime Ministers in the UK and their equivalents elsewhere, who should use their values to inform goals and ambitions, but rely on valid expert analysis and robust evidence for their tactics and methods of implementation (Perry et al. 2010).

# Chapter 6 – So what have we learnt about successful routes for evidence-into-use?

So far, a total of 30 relevant studies (or reviews that include such studies) have been found, with 38 distinct approaches evaluated within them. Many are not of very high quality, but unlike the merely descriptive work all have at least a counterfactual design or suitable comparator or similar. Tables 6.1 to 6.4 show the citation, general area of public policy/practice, and whether the results are positive, negative (no impact or harmful), or unclear, for each approach evaluated. Table 6.1 summarises the research estimated to be of quality 4 using the sieve approach (see above). Tables 6.2 to 6.4 show the results for quality 3, 2, and 1 respectively.

This summary shows that much more robust evaluation work has been conducted on practice (across all fields) than on policy, and more in health than education or any other area. There is nothing specifically on education policy-making at all. This means that much of the improved evidence generated in the past 20 years could have been wasted or at least not used most effectively because, as a society, we have so little idea how to put evidence-into-use. Education policy is still not generally informed by evidence, but more so by politics, beliefs and the views of funders (Slavin 2017). This is true of policy more widely, even where decisions are clearly meant to be evidence-based (Dick et al. 2016). Users do not usually act in accordance with evidence even where this is freely available to them (Epstein 2017). The findings of high quality substantive research have not become embedded in policy or practice, while too much lower quality evidence is still being promoted (Gorard 2018).

There is no evidence that approaches like cell a, b, or e are useful, and indications that they are not the way to improve the uptake of evidence. There is almost no evidence for cells g and I, despite their apparent promise. The work involving cell d gives very mixed results. Cells c, h and especially f are the most promising.

Table 6.1 – Summary of evaluations of evidence-into-use rated 4

| Study | Target area | Positive effect | Inconclusive | Negative or harmful |
|---|---|---|---|---|
| Elouafkaoui et al. 2016 | Dental practice | cell f | | |
| NFER 2017 | Education practice | | | cell d cell e |

Table 6.2 – Summary of evaluations of evidence-into-use rated 3

| Study | Target area | Positive effect | Inconclusive | Negative or harmful |
|---|---|---|---|---|
| Bero et al. 1998 | Health practice | | | cell a cell d |
| Menon et al. 2009 | Health practice | cell f | | |
| Murthy et al. 2012 | Health practice | | cell e | |
| Petkovic et al. 2010 | Policy (general) | | cell d | |
| Rohwer et al. 2017 | Health practice | | cell d | |
| Siddiqi et al. 2005 | Health practice | cell f | cell e | cell d |
| University of Bristol 2017 | Education practice | | | cell e |

Table 6.3 – Summary of evaluations of evidence-into-use
rated 2

| Study | Target area | Positive effect | Inconclu sive | Negative or harmful |
|---|---|---|---|---|
| Abdullah et al. 2014 | Health practice | | cell e | |
| Buljan et al. 2017 | Health education | | cell d | |
| Dobbins et al. 2009b | Health practice | | cell h | cell e |
| Forsetlund et al. 2003 | Health practice | | cell f | |
| Gordon et al. 2005 | Dental practice | cell d cell f | | |
| Lewis et al. 2005 | Health practice | | cell e | |
| See et al. 2016 | Education practice | | | cell c |
| Taylor et al. 2004 | Health practice | | cell b | |
| Yost et al. 2015 | Health practice | | | cell e |
| Wyatt et al. 1998 | Health practice | | | cell b |

Of course, which cell any study appears in relies on a judgment, but the summary here is reasonably robust, at least for evidence into practice – both in terms of route and quality of the evaluations of each route. In order to be most effective, evidence has to be modified/engineered, to some considerable extent, into a more useful format. And it cannot simply be made available to users. There has to be active engagement in the translation of evidence into use.

Table 6.4 – Summary of evaluations of evidence-into-use rated 1

| Study | Target area | Positive effect | Inconclu sive | Negative or harmful |
|---|---|---|---|---|
| Barwick et al. 2009 | Health practice | | | cell f |
| Davis and Taylor-Vaisey 1997 | Health practice | cell f cell h | | cell e |
| Di Noia et al. 2003 | Health practice | | cell d | |
| Griggs et al. 2016 | Education practice | | cell e | |
| Gülmezoglu et al. 2007 | Health practice | | | cell b |
| Rosenbaum et al. 2004 | Health practice | cell d | | |
| Ruangkanchana setr 1993 | Health practice | | cell f | |
| Seers at al. 2004 | Health practice | | | cell d |
| Speight et al. 2016 | Education practice | | cell e | |
| Thompson et al. 2007 | Health practice | | cell e | |
| Tranmer et al. 2002 | Health practice | cell c | | |

There is very little work on the use of research evidence that has been carefully crafted (engineered) into more usable or accessible forms. Again, there is no reason to believe that simply making such evidence-led products available will be effective. They will be competing with commercial and other products which will make comparable but often unwarranted claims. The user is not in a good position to check which of such products is really based on solid evidence (see above). The one study with a positive outcome suggests that a developer or other agent still has to engage with users to get the engineered evidence into use.

Population measures, such as legislation or structural change, remain promising ways of getting evidence-based approaches into use – but such measures are currently too often not evidence-based. So even with these, the question remains – how is it possible to get the policy-maker or practitioner to recognise and use the best evidence or even to use evidence at all?

A further distinction, other than the two dimensions of modification of evidence and engagement in dissemination, concerns the level of outcomes assessed by each study. Some looked at whether there was a change in the knowledge or awareness of research evidence for the user, or whether the user changed their attitude to the use of evidence. Some looked more directly at whether users changed their actual behaviour in relation to evidence-led actions (by prescribing or teaching differently, for example). Some, most usefully, tested whether evidence-use made any difference to end-user outcomes, such as whether there were improved results for students or patients. And some studies looked at a combination of these. We consider the results for each type of outcome in turn.

*Attitude/awareness outcomes*

The majority of work looked primarily at awareness/attitude outcomes, and this includes the only piece concerning policy (Table 6.5). Only four approaches or interventions were deemed successful, and two of these were the result of rather weak evaluations. All four involved modified or engineered evidence, and three of them involved considerable engagement in dissemination. There is no 4* work on awareness/attitude outcomes. Much of the rest is inconclusive or evenly balanced in quality between positive and negative. The balance of research quality and direction of reported outcomes from these studies is not as skewed as it has been for all other reviews we have conducted (e.g. Gorard et al. 2016b).

Table 6.5 – Summary of awareness/attitude outcomes

| Study | Quality | Positive effect | Inconclusive | Negative/harmful |
|---|---|---|---|---|
| Menon et al. 2009 | 3* | cell f | | |
| Bero et al. 1998 | 3* | | | cell a, d |
| Murthy et al. 2012 | 3* | | cell e | |
| Petkovic et al. 2010 | 3* | | cell d | |
| *Rohwer et al. 2017* | 3* | | cell d | |
| Abdullah et al. | 2* | | cell e | |
| Buljan et al. 2017 | 2* | | cell d | |
| Dobbins et al. 2009b | 2* | | cell h | cell e |
| Forsetlund et al. 2003 | 2* | | cell f | |
| Taylor et al. 2004 | 2* | | cell b | |
| Yost et al. 2015 | 2* | | | cell e |
| Davis and Taylor-Vaisey 1997 | 1* | cell f, h | | cell e |
| Barwick et al. 2009 | 1* | | cell f | |
| Di Noia et al. 2003 | 1* | | cell d | |
| Rosenbaum et al. 2004 | 1* | cell d | | |
| Thompson et al. 2007 | 1* | | cell e | |

Table 6.6 gives a breakdown of the results in Table 6.5 in terms of each of the nine cells – the routes to evidence-use. Some routes have been tested much more than others. The review found little or nothing to endorse the value of simply making raw evidence available when trying to change attitudes to, or awareness of, research. This is a cheap and easy approach, but unlikely to be effective except in peculiar circumstances. In fact, there is no good evidence that using raw evidence and expecting it to make any difference will ever work. This is largely because so little even respectably robust work has been done. Results suggest that in trying to make users more aware of or more favourable to the use of evidence, neither passive approaches nor plain access to evidence is enough. Evidence needs to be modified at least to some extent, and presented actively and often iteratively.

Table 6.6 – Comparing routes to evidence-use and direction of awareness/attitude outcomes, number of studies

| Cell | Positive | Inconclusive | Negative |
|------|----------|--------------|----------|
| a – plain, passive | - | - | 1 |
| b – plain, engaged | - | 2 | - |
| c – plain, active | - | - | - |
| d – modified, passive | 1 | 4 | 1 |
| e – modified, engaged | - | 3 | 3 |
| f – modified, active | 2 | 2 | - |
| g – engineered, passive | - | - | - |
| h – engineered, engaged | 1 | 1 | - |
| i – engineered, active | - | - | - |

*Change in behaviour/practice outcomes*

There are no policy-related studies with behaviour outcomes (Table 6.7). However, this kind of outcome does have some of the strongest evidence found in the review. Cell f is the most promising – using modified evidence and active dissemination to change practice behaviour (Table 6.8). Cell b is probably the least promising. The only positive outcome study based on using plain evidence was among the weakest found, with a very small cell size (10 nurses in the smallest group). Otherwise, the studies are again spread between positive, negative and unclear results from different quality evaluations.

Table 6.77 – Summary of high/medium quality evaluations with user behaviour outcomes

| Study | Research quality | Positive effect | Inconclusive | Negative or harmful |
|---|---|---|---|---|
| Elouafkaoui et al. 2016 | 4* | cell f | | |
| NFER 2017 | 4* | | | cell d, e |
| Siddiqi et al. 2005 | 3* | cell f | cell e | cell d |
| Gordon et al. 2005 | 2* | cell d, f | | |
| Lewis et al. 2005 | 2* | | cell e | |
| Wyatt et al. 1998 | 2* | | | cell b |
| Griggs et al. 2016 | 1* | | cell e | |
| Gülmezoglu et al. 2007 | 1* | | | cell b |
| Ruangkanchana setr 1993 | 1* | | cell f | |
| Seers et al. 2004 | 1* | | | cell d |
| Speight et al. 2016 | 1* | | cell e | |
| Tranmer et al. 2002 | 1* | cell c | | |

Table 6.8 – Comparing routes to evidence-use and direction of user behaviour outcomes, number of studies

| Cell | Positive | Inconclusive | Negative |
|---|---|---|---|
| a – plain, passive | - | - | - |
| b – plain, engaged | - | - | 2 |
| c – plain, active | 1 | - | - |
| d – modified, passive | 1 | - | 3 |
| e – modified, engaged | - | 4 | 1 |
| f – modified, active | 3 | 1 | - |
| g – engineered, passive | - | - | - |
| h – engineered, engaged | - | - | - |
| i – engineered, active | - | - | - |

*End-user outcomes*

All of the studies that actually attempt to measure the impact of evidence-use on measureable outcomes for the intended end-users of policy/practice, such as improved student test results, are in education. They are of reasonably high quality, and show that these routes for evidence into use make no difference (Table 6.9). Modified evidence with passive delivery of research results does not impact on end-user outcomes, nor does minimal engagement with users, even when the research findings are modified into a more useable format (Table 6.10). Of course, the number of studies is still small but it does suggest that current approaches need a radical rethink.

Table 6.9 – Summary of high/medium quality evaluations with end-user impact outcomes

| Study | Researc h quality | Positiv e effect | Inconclusiv e | Negativ e or harmful |
|---|---|---|---|---|
| NFER 2017 | 4* | - | - | cell d, e |
| Universit y of Bristol 2017 | 3* | - | - | cell e |
| See et al. 2016 | 2* | | | cell c |

Table 6.10 – Comparing routes to evidence-use and direction of end-user impact outcomes, number of studies

| Cell | Positive | Inconclusive | Negative |
|------|----------|--------------|----------|
| a – plain, passive | - | - | - |
| b – plain, engaged | - | - | - |
| c – plain, active | - | - | 1 |
| d – modified, passive | - | - | 1 |
| e – modified, engaged | - | - | 2 |
| f – modified, active | - | - | - |
| g – engineered, passive | - | - | - |
| h – engineered, engaged | - | - | - |
| i – engineered, active | - | - | - |

## Chapter 7 - Implications and conclusions

As with any attempt to change or improve behaviour, the role of money could be key in encouraging the use of evidence in policy/practice. Those who fund education research need to be responsible with the money they are entrusted with by tax-payers or charity-givers. The research they fund must be as high quality as possible, and the findings must be made as useful as possible. This is currently not happening. The most common approach used by funders to promote the use of evidence is to insist that users are linked to any project. Yet they are unable to provide any serious evidence that this approach is effective (McLean et al. 2018).

Clearly, the preparation and continuing development of teachers should have an evidence-led basis, which too often it currently does not. Here is another area where funding could play a role. Initial teacher training courses must be delivered, at least in part, by experts in education evidence. And the state should only fund them, and recognise their qualifications, if they are.

Policy and practice interventions should always be independently evaluated before reform takes place, instead of using rather haphazard pilots and phased rollout. Clear objectives must be pre-specified, and side effects taken into account. Incentives could be used, at least in the short term, to encourage users to rely more on evidence, and for the public to demand this (Miller et al. 2006, Rutter 2012). Public funds could be shifted towards only paying for programmes that have been demonstrated independently to have strong promise (Pew Charitable Trusts 2014, Hess and Little 2015). Good evidence of effectiveness should be transparent in all policy and practice decisions about new programmes, and only those that offer a good return should be funded. A central repository of effective programmes should be built up by funders or others (and not just for teaching in schools). In the same way that any area of research should start with a full review of existing evidence, so new results should also be placed clearly and coherently in the context of that prior evidence. Each new result should add to a kind of narrative "Bayesian" synthesis, considering how new research changes what we already think we know about in the repository, rather than seeking to have use and impact in its own right.

Those in charge of education reform must be responsible, and demand evidence-led policy and practice throughout the system. Programmes shown not to work, or where there has been no robust evaluation, should be actively discouraged, given that there is growing evidence of programmes that do seem to work. Researchers need to be equally responsible, and resist the clear demand for their evidence to be used, even if it is used incorrectly, by not conniving with invalid use just so that they can claim 'impact'. These are all largely ethical issues, concerning the extent to which all of these stakeholders genuinely care about improving education.

# References

Aarons, G., Hurlburt, M. and Horwitz, S. (2011) Advancing a conceptual model of evidence-based practice implementation in public service sectors, *Administration and Policy in Mental Health and Mental Health Services Research, 38*, 1, 4-23

Abbott, P. McSherry, R. and Simmons, M. (2013) *Evidence-informed nursing: A guide for clinical nurses*, Routledge

Abdullah, G., Rossy, D., Poeg, J., Davies. B., Higuchi, K., Sikora, L. and Stacey, D. (2014) Measuring the effectiveness of mentoring as a knowledge translation intervention, *Worldviews on Evidence-based Nursing*, 11, 5, 284-300

Ademokun, A., Dennis, A., Hayter, E., Richards, C., Runceanu, L, Cassidy, C., Liebnitzky, J., Suliman, S., and Kovacs, M. (2016) *Evidence-informed policymaking toolkit*, Oxford: INASP

Admiraal, W., Buijs, M., Claessens, W., Honing,T. and Karkdijk. J. (2016) Linking theory and practice: teacher research in history and geography classrooms, *Educational Action Research*, 1-16

Al Hallami, M., and Brown, C. (2014) Scenarios of London Local Authorities' Engagement with Evidence Bases for Education Policies, *Issues in Educational Research*, 24, 2, 117-132

Alliance for Useful Evidence (2014) *How to get policymakers to use more evidence - a systematic review*, https://www.alliance4usefulevidence.org/how-to-get-policymakers-to-use-more-evidence/

Alliance for Useful Evidence and Cabinet Office (2017) What Works Centre Network, http://www.alliance4usefulevidence.org/event/what-works-centres-network-open-day/

Alton-Lee, A. (2011) (Using) Evidence for Educational Improvement, *Cambridge Journal of Education*, 41, 3, 303-329

Apollonio, D. and Bero, L (2017) Interpretation and use of evidence in state policymaking: a qualitative analysis, *BMJ* 7, 2

Arinder, M. (2016) Bridging the divide between evidence and policy in public sector decision making, *Public Administration Review*, 76, 3, 394-398

ATL (2013) *Using evidence to inform education policy and practice*, ATL

Barwick, M., Peters, J. and Boydell, K. (2009) Getting to uptake: Do communities of practice support the implementation of evidence-based practice?, *Journal of the Canadian Academy of Child and Adolescent Psychiatry*, 18, 16-29

Baumbusch, J., Kirkham, S., Khan, K., McDonald, H., Semeniuk, P., Tan, E. and Anderson, J. (2008) Pursuing common agendas: a collaborative model for knowledge translation between research and practice in clinical settings, *Research in Nursing & Health*, 31, 2, 130-140

Bell, S. and Peck, L. (2016) On the feasibility of extending social experiments to wider applications, *Journal of MultiDisciplinary Evaluation*, 12, 27, 93-112

Benmarhnia, T., Huang, J. and Jones, C. (2017) Lost in translation: piloting a novel framework to assess the challenges in translating scientific uncertainty, *International Journal of Health Policy & Management*, 6, 11, 649-660

Bergman, D. (1999) Evidence-based guidelines an critical pathways for quality improvement, *Pediatrics*, 103(Supplement E1), 225-232

Bero, L., Grilli, R., Grimshaw, J., Harvey, E., Oxman, A. and Thomson, M. (1998) Closing the gap between research and practice: an overview of systematic reviews of interventions to promote the implementation of research findings: The Cochrane Effective Practice and Organization of Care Review Group, *BMJ (Clinical Research Ed.)*, *317*, 7156, 465-468

Bertram, M., Loncarevic, N., Radl-Karimi, C., Thogersen, M., Skovgaard, T. and Aro, A. (2018) Contextually tailored interventions can increase evidence-informed policymaking on health-enhancing physical activitiy: the experiences of two Danish municipalities, *Health Research Policy and Systems*, 16(14)

Biesta, G. (2010) Why 'What Works' still Won't Work: From evidence-based education to value-Based education, *Studies in Philosophy and Education*, 29, 5, 491-503

Black, N. (2001) Evidence based policy: Proceed with care, *BMJ*, 323(7307), 275-278

Blanden, J., Gregg, P. and Machin, S. (2005) *Intergenerational mobility in Europe and North America: Report for the Sutton Trust*, London: Centre for Economic Performance, http://cep.lse.ac.uk/about/news/IntergenerationalMobility.pdf

Blase, K., Fixsen, D. and Jackson, K. (2015) *Creating meaningful change in education: A cascading logic model*, Scaling-Up Brief 6, http://search.ebscohost.com/login.aspx?direct=true&db=eric&AN=ED576693&site=ehost-live

Bogenschneider, K., Little, O. and Johnson. K. (2013) Policymakers' Use of Social Science Research: Looking Within and Across Policy Actors, *Journal of Marriage and Family,* 75, 2, 263-275

Bowen, S. and Zwi, A. (2005) Pathways to "Evidence-Informed" policy and practice: A framework for action, *PLoS Med*, 2, 7, e166

Boydell, K.., Dew, A., Hodgins, M., Bundy, A., Gallego, G., Iljadica, A., . . . Willis, D. (2017) Deliberative dialogues between policy makers and researchers in Canada and Australia, *Journal of Disability Policy Studies*, 28, 1, 13-22

Brandy, R. Maynard, R. and Nathaniel A. Dell (2018) Use and Impacts of Campbell Systematic Reviews on Policy, Practice, and Research, *Research on Social Work Practice*, 28, 1, 13-18

Brehaut, J. and Juzwishin, D. (2005) *Bridging the gap: the use of research evidence in policy development,* Health Technology Assessment initiative Series, http://www.crd.york.ac.uk/CRDWeb/ShowRecord.asp?ID=32005001181

Brennan, S., Cumpston, M., Misso, M., McDonald, S., Murphy, M. and Green, S. (2016) Design and formative evaluation of the Policy Liaison Initiative: a long-term knowledge translation strategy to encourage and support the use of Cochrane systematic reviews for informing health policy, *Evidence and Policy*, 12, 1, 25-52

Brown, C. (2012a) Adoption by policy makers of knowledge from educational research: An alternative perspective, *Issues in Educational Research*, 22, 2, 91-110

Brown, C. (2012b) Exploring the concepts of knowledge adoption and conceptual impact: implications for educational research submissions to the Research Excellence Framework 2014, *Education, Knowledge and Economy*, 5, 3, 137-154

Brown, C. (2014) Advancing policy makers' expertise in evidence-use: A new approach to enhancing the role research can have in aiding educational policy development, *Journal of Educational Change*, 15, 19–36

Brown, C. and Rogers, S. (2015) Measuring the effectiveness of knowledge creation activity as a means to facilitate evidence-informed practice: a study of early years' settings in Camden, London, *Evidence and Policy: A Journal of Research, Debate and Practice*, 11, 2, 189-207

Brown, C., Wickline, M., Ecoff, L. and Glaser, D. (2009) Nursing practice, knowledge, attitudes and perceived barriers to evidence-based practice at an academic medical center, *Journal of Advanced Nursing*, 65, 2, 371-381

Brownson, R. (2017) *Dissemination and implementation research in health: translating science to practice,* Oxford: Oxford University Press

Brownson, R., Dodson, E., Stamatakis, K., Casey, C., Elliott, M., Luke, D., Wintrode, M. and Kreuter, W. (2011) Communicating evidence-based information on cancer prevention to state-level policy makers, *Journal of the National Cancer Institute*, 103, 4, 306-316

Buljan, I., Malički, M., Wager, E., Puljak, L. Hren, D., Kellie, F., West, H., Alfirević, Z. and Marušić, A. (2017) No difference in knowledge obtained from infographic or plain language summary of a Cochrane systematic review: three randomized controlled trials, *Journal of Clinical Epidemiology*, http://dx.doi.org/10.1016/j.jclinepi.2017.12.003

Burstein, P. (2003) The impact of public opinion on public policy: A review and an agenda, *Political Research Quarterly*, 56, 1, 29-40

Cacari-Stone, L., Wallerstein, N., Garcia, A. and Minkler, M. (2014) The promise of community-based participatory research for health equity: a conceptual model for bridging evidence with policy, *American Journal of Public Health*, *104*, 9, 1615-1623

CAHO (2008) *The case for evidence-based policy: looking at the impact of the Ontario drug policy research network*, http://caho-hospitals.com/the-case-for-evidence-based-policy-looking-at-the-impact-of-the-ontario-drug-policy-research-network-odprn/

Cain, T. (2019) Don't be a research fundamentalist, *TES*, 25/1/19, https://www.tes.com/news/tes-magazine/tes-magazine/dont-be-a-research-fundamentalist

Cain, T. (2015) Teachers' engagement with published research: addressing the knowledge problem, *The Curriculum Journal*, 26, 3, 488-509

Cain, T. and Allan, D. (2017) The invisible impact of educational research, *Oxford Review of Education*, 10.1080/03054985.2017.1316252

California Department of Education (n.d.) *Evidence-based interventions under the ESSA*, https://www.cde.ca.gov/re/es/evidence.asp

Cambridge Public Policy (2017) *How to evidence and record policy impact*, https://www.publicpolicy.cam.ac.uk/pdf/policy-impact-april-2017

Cameron, A., Salisbury, C., Lart, R., Stewart, K., Peckham, S., Calnan, M., . . . Thorp, H. (2011) Policy makers' perceptions on the use of evidence from evaluations, *Evidence & Policy: A Journal of Research, Debate and Practice*, 7, 4, 429-447

Campbell, D., Donald, B., Moore, G. and Frew, D. (2011) Evidence Check: knowledge brokering to commission research reviews for policy, *Evidence and Policy*, 7, 1, 97-107

Carrier, N. (2017) How educational ideas catch on: the promotion of popular education innovations and the role of evidence, *Educational Research*, 59, 2

Castellani, T., Valente, A., Cori, L. and Bianchi, F. (2016). Detecting the use of evidence in a meta-policy, *Evidence & Policy: A Journal of Research, Debate and Practice*, 12, 1, 91-107

Castleman, B. (2015) *Knowing when to nudge*, Brown Center, https://www.brookings.edu/blog/brown-center-chalkboard/2015/08/06/knowing-when-to-nudge-in-education

Chaloupka, F. and Johnston, L. (2007) Bridging the gap: Research informing practice and policy for healthy youth behaviour, *American Journal of Preventive Medicine*, 33, 4, Suppl, S147-S161, doi:10.1016/j.amepre.2007.07.016

Chambers, D., Wilson, P., Thompson, C., Hanbury, A., Farley, K. and Light, K. (2011) Maximizing the impact of systematic reviews in health care decision making: a systematic scoping review of knowledge-translation resources, *The Milbank Quarterly*, 89, 1, 131-156

Chaudoir, S., Dugan, A. and Barr, C. (2013) Measuring factors affecting implementation of health innovations: a systematic review of structural, organizational, provider, patient, and innovation level measures, *Implementation Science*, 8, 1, 22

Chubb, J. and Watermeyer, R. (2017) Artifice or integrity in the marketplace of research impact?, *Studies in Higher Education*, 14, 2, 2360-2372

Churches, R. (2016) *Closing the gap: test and learn* (Research report DFE-RR500b), Nottingham: National College for Teaching and Leadership

Clarkson J., Ramsay, C., Eccles, M., Eldridge, S., Grimshaw, J. *et al.* (2010) The translation research in a dental setting (TRiaDS) programme protocol, *Implementation Science*, 5, 57, 10.1186/1748-5908-5-57

Coburn, C., Penuel, W. and Geil, K. (2013) *Research-practice partnerships: A strategy for leveraging research for educational improvement in school districts,* William T. Grant Foundation, New York, NY

Cohen, D., Crabtree, B., Etz, R., Balasubramanian, B., Donahue, K., Leviton, L., ... Green, L (2008) Fidelity versus flexibility: translating evidence-based research into practice, *American Journal of Preventive Medicine*, 35, 5, S381-S389

Coldwell, M., Greany, T., Higgins, S., Brown, C., Maxwell, B., Stiell, B., Stoll, L., Willis, B. and Burns, H. (2017) *Evidence-informed teaching: an evaluation of progress* (DFE-RR-696) London: DfE

Collins, K. (2018) *Going global,* https://educationendowmentfoundation.org.uk/news/go ing-global-scaling-up-evidence-to-the-international/?mc_cid=09c0b25e5b&mc_eid=ba4641e 5ba

Connell, J. and Klem, A. (2000) You can get there from here: Using a theory of change approach to plan urban education reform, *Journal of Educational and Psychological Consultation*, 11, 1, 93-120

Connelly, S., Vanderhoven, D., Durose, C., Richardson, L., Matthews, P. and Rutherfoord, R. (2016) Translation across borders: Exploring the use, relevance and impact of academic research in the policy process, in D. O'Brien and Matthews, P.(Eds.) *After urban regeneration: Communities, policy and place* (pp. 181-198), Connected Communities series, Bristol and

Chicago: Policy Press; distributed by University of Chicago Press

Cook, P., & Ludwig, J. (2006) Aiming for Evidence-Based Gun Policy, *Journal of Policy Analysis and Management*, 25, 3, 691-735

Cooper, A., Levin, B. and Campbell, C. (2009) The growing (but still limited) importance of evidence in education policy and practice, *J Educ Change*, 10, 159–171

Corcoran, T. (2003) *The use of research evidence in instructional improvement*, CPRE Policy Briefs RB-40, http://search.ebscohost.com/login.aspx?direct=true&db =eric&AN=ED498344&site=ehost-live

Corrigan, P., Steiner, L., McCracken, S., Blaser, B. and Barr, M. (2001) Strategies for disseminating evidence-based practices to staff who treat people with serious mental illness, *Psychiatric Services*, 52, 12, 1598-1606

Coutts, P. and Orlik, E. (2017) *Learning from the What Works Network*, http://www.alliance4usefulevidence.org/learning-from-the-what-works-network/

Cowen, N. (2019) For whom does 'what works' work? The political economy of evidence-based education, *Educational Research and Evaluation*, http://www.academia.edu/37248352/For_whom_does_ what_works_work_The_political_economy_of_eviden ce-based_education

Crocco, M., Halvorsen, A., Jacobsen, R. and Segall, A. (2017) Teaching with evidence, *Phi Delta Kappan*, 98, 7, 67-71

Curtis, K., Fry, M., Shaban R. and Considine, J. (2017)Translating research findings to clinical nursing practice, *Journal of Clinical Nursing*, 26, 862–872, doi: 10.1111/jocn.13586

Dagenais, C., Queuille, L. and Ridde, V. (2013) Evaluation of a knowledge transfer strategy from a user fee exemption program for vulnerable populations in Burkina Faso, *Global Health Promotion*, 20, 1 suppl, 70-79

Daly, A., Finnigan, K., Jordan, S., Moolenaar, N. and Che, J. (2014) Misalignment and perverse incentives:

Examining the politics of district leaders as brokers in the use of research evidence, *Educational Policy*, 28, 2, 145-174

Damschroder, L., Aron, D., Keith, R., Kirsh, S., Alexander, J. and Lowery, J. (2009) Fostering implementation of health services research findings into practice: a consolidated framework for advancing implementation science, *Implementation Science*, 4, 1, 50

Daugherty, R. (2008) Reviewing national curriculum assessment in Wales: how can evidence inform the development of policy?, *Cambridge Journal of Education*, 38, 1, 73-87

Davies, P. (1999) What is evidence-based education?, *British Journal of Educational Studies*, 47, 2, 108-121

Davies, P. (2012) The state of evidence-based policy evaluation and its role in policy formation, *National Institute Economic Review*, 219, 1, R41-R52

Davis, D. and Taylor-Vaisey, A. (1997) Translating guidelines into practice: a systematic review of theoretic concepts, practical experience and research evidence in the adoption of clinical practice guidelines, *Canadian Medical Association Journal*, *157*, 4, 408-416

Davis, D., Davis, M. , Jadad, A., Perrier, L., Rath, D., Ryan, D., ... Zwarenstein, M. (2003) The case for knowledge translation: shortening the journey from evidence to effect, *BMJ*, *327*, 7405, 33-35

Di Noia, J., Schwinn, T., Dastur, Z. and Schinke, S. (2003) The relative efficacy of pamphlets, CD-ROM, and the Internet for disseminating adolescent drug abuse prevention programs: an exploratory study, *Preventative Medicine*, 37, 646-653

Dick, A., Rich, W. and Waters, T. (2016) Prison vocational education and policy in the United States, New York: Palgrave Macmillan

Dimmock, C. (2016) Conceptualising the research–practice–professional development nexus: mobilising schools as 'research-engaged' professional learning communities, *Professional Development in Education*, 42, 1, 36-53

Dingfelder, H. and Mandell, D. (2011) Bridging the research-to-practice gap in autism intervention: An application of diffusion of innovation theory, *Journal of Autism and Developmental Disorders, 41*, 5, 597-609

Dobbins M., Hanna S., Ciliska D., Manske S., Cameron R., Mercer SL., O'Mara L., DeCorby K. and Robeson P. (2009b) A randomized controlled trial evaluating the impact of knowledge translation and exchange strategies, *Implementation Science, 23*, 4, 61

Dobbins, M., Cockerill, R. and Barnsley, J. (2001) Factors affecting the utilization of systematic reviews. A study of public health decision makers, *International Journal of Technology Assessment in Health Care, 17*, 2, 203-14

Dobbins, M., Robeson, P., Ciliska, D., Hanna, S., Cameron, R., O'Mara, L., ... Mercer, S. (2009a) A description of a knowledge broker role implemented as part of a randomized controlled trial evaluating three knowledge translation strategies, *Implementation Science, 4*, 1, 23

Dodson, E., Geary, N. and Brownson, R. (2015) State legislators' sources and use of information: bridging the gap between research and policy, *Health Education Research, 30*, 6, 840-848

Drill, K., Miller, S., Behrstock-Sherratt, E. (2012) *Teachers' Perspectives on Educational Research* American Institutes for Research, Napierville, IL, http://files.eric.ed.gov/fulltext/ED530742.pdf

Dufault M., Bielecki C., Collins E. and Willey C. (1995) Changing nurses' pain assessment practice: a collaborative research utilization approach, *J Adv Nurs*, 21, 634-645

Dwan, K., McInnes, P. and Mazumdar, S. (2015) Measuring the success of facilitated engagement between knowledge producers and users: a validated scale, *Evidence and Policy*, 11, 2, 239-252

Edwards, M. (2010) Making research more relevant to policy evidence and suggestions, in Bammer, G., Michaux, A. and Sanson, A. (Eds.) *Bridging the 'Know-Do' Gap* (pp. 55-64), ANU Press

EEF (2018) *IPEELL: using self-regulation to improve writing* (re-grant), https://educationendowmentfoundation.org.uk/projects -and- evaluation/projects/ipeell?mc_cid=febc011cb7&mc_ei d=ba4641e5ba

EEF (2018) *Putting evidence to work*, https://educationendowmentfoundation.org.uk/index.p hp?/tools/guidance-reports/a-schools-guide-to- implementation/

El-Jardali, F., Lavis, J., Ataya, N. and Jamal, D. (2012) Use of health systems and policy research in the health policymaking in eastern Mediterranean countries: views and practices of researchers, *Implementation Science*, 7, 2

El-Jardali, F., Lavis, J., Moat, K., Pantoja, T. and Ataya, N. (2014) Capturing lessons learned from evidence-policy initiatives through structured reflection, *Health Research Policy and Systems*, 12, 2

Ellen, M., Horowitz, E., Vaknin. S. and Lavis. J. (2016a) View of health system policymakers on the role of research in health policymaking in Israel, *Israel Journal of Health Policy Research*, 5, 24

Ellen, M., Lavis, J. and Shemer, J. (2016b) Examining the use of health systems and policy research in health policymaking process in Israel: views of researchers, *Health Research Policy and Systems*, 14, 1

Ellen, M., Lavis, J., Horowitz, E. and Berglas, R. (2018) How is the use of research evidence in health policy perceived? A comparison between the reporting of researchers and policy-makers, *Health Research Policy and Systems*, 16, 64

Elliott, H. and Popay, J. (2000) How are policy makers using evidence? Models of research utilisation and local NHS policy making, *Journal of Epidemiology and Community Health*, 54, 6, 461-468

Ellis, P., Robinson, P., Ciliska, D., Armour, T., Brouwers, M., O'Brien, M. A., . . . Raina, P. (2005) A systematic review of studies evaluating diffusion and dissemination of selected cancer control interventions, *Health Psychology, 24*, 5, 488-500

Elouafkaoui, P., Young L., Newlands R., Duncan E., Elders A., Clarkson J. et al. (2016) An audit and feedback intervention for reducing antibiotic prescribing in general dental practice, *PLOS Med* 13, 8

Epstein, D. *(2017) When evidence says no, but doctors say yes, ProPublica,*
https://www.theatlantic.com/health/archive/2017/02/when-evidence-says-no-but-doctors-say-yes/517368/

Farley-Ripple, E., May, H., Karpyn, A., Tilley, K., & McDonough, K. (2018). Rethinking Connections Between Research and Practice in Education: A Conceptual Framework. *Educational Researcher*, 0013189X18761042

Feldstein, A. and Glasgow, R. (2008) A practical, robust implementation and sustainability model (PRISM) for integrating research findings into practice, *The Joint Commission Journal on Quality and Patient Safety, 34*, 4, 228-243

Fineout-Overholt, E., Levin, R. and Melnyk, B. (2004) Strategies for advancing evidence-based practice in clinical settings, *JNY State Nurses Assoc, 35*, 2, 28-32

Fink, R., Thompson, C. and Bonnes, D. (2005) Overcoming barriers and promoting the use of research in practice, *Journal of Nursing Administration, 35*, 3, 121-129

Finnigan, K., Daly, A. and Che, J. (2013) Systemwide reform in districts under pressure The role of social networks in defining, acquiring, using, and diffusing research evidence, *Journal of Educational Administration, 51*, 4, 476-497

Forsetlund, L., Talseth, K., Bradley, P., Nordheim, L. and Bjorndal, A. (2003) Many a slip between cup and lip. Process evaluation of a program to promote and support evidence-based public health practice, *Evaluation Review*, 27, 179-209

Fraser, C., Herman, J., Elgie, S. and Childs, R. (2018) How school leaders search for and use evidence, *Educational*

*Research,*
https://www.tandfonline.com/doi/full/10.1080/001318
81.2018.1533791

French, S., Green, S., O'Connor, D., McKenzie, J., Francis, J., Michie, S., ... Grimshaw, J. (2012) Developing theory-informed behaviour change interventions to implement evidence into practice: a systematic approach using the Theoretical Domains Framework, *Implementation Science,* 7, 1, 38

Friese, B. and Bogenschneider, K. (2009) The Voice of Experience: How social scientists communicate family research to policymakers, *Family Relations,* 58, 2, 229-243

Galway, G. and Sheppard, B. (2015) Research and evidence in education decision-making: A comparison of results from two pan-Canadian studies, *Education Policy Analysis Archives* 23, 108/109, 1-37

Gardner, J., Holmes, B. and Leitch, R. (2008) Where there is smoke, there is (the potential for) fire: Soft indicators of research and policy impact, *Cambridge Journal of Education,* 38, 1, 89-104

Garner, P., Kale, R., Dickson, R., Dans, T. and Salinas, R. (1998) Getting research findings into practice: Implementing research findings in developing countries, *BMJ,* 317, 7157, 531-535

Gerrish, K. and Clayton, J. (2004) Promoting evidence-based practice: an organizational approach, *Journal of Nursing Management,* 12, 2, 114-123

Giles-Corti, B., Sallis, J. F., Sugiyama, T., Frank, L., Lowe, M. and Owen, N. (2015) Translating active living research into policy and practice: one important pathway to chronic disease prevention, *Journal of Public Health Policy,* 36, 2, 231-243

Glasgow, R. and Emmons, K. (2007) How can we increase translation of research into practice? Types of evidence needed, *Annual Review of Public Health,* 28, 413-433

Glasgow, R., Lichtenstein, E. and Marcus, A. (2003) Why don't we see more translation of health promotion research to practice? Rethinking the efficacy-to-effectiveness transition, *American Journal of Public Health*, *93*, 8, 1261-1267

Gollust, S., Kite, H., Benning, S., Callanan, R., Weisman, S., & Nanney, M. (2014) Use of research evidence in state policymaking for childhood obseity prevention in Minnesota, *American Journal of Public Health*, 104, 10, 1894-1900

Gonzales, R., Handley, M., Ackerman, S. and O'Sullivan, P. (2012) Increasing the translation of evidence into practice, policy, and public health improvements, *Academic Medicine*, 87, 3, 271--278

Gorard, S. (2006) *Using everyday numbers effectively in research*, London: Continuum

Gorard, S. (2013) *Research Design: Robust approaches for the social sciences*, London: SAGE

Gorard, S. (2018) *Education policy: Evidence of equity and effectiveness*, Bristol: Policy Press

Gorard, S. and See, BH and Morris, R. (2016b) *The most effective approaches to teaching in primary schools*, Saarbrucken: Lambert Academic Publishing

Gorard, S. and Siddiqui, N. (2018a) There *is* only research: the liberating impact of just doing research, *International Journal of Multiple Research Approaches*, 10, 1, 328-333

Gorard, S. and Siddiqui, N. (2018b) Grammar schools in England: a new analysis of social segregation and academic outcomes, *British Journal of Sociology of Education*, 39, 7, 909-924

Gorard, S., Rushforth, K. and Taylor, C. (2004) Is there a shortage of quantitative work in education research?, *Oxford Review of Education*, 30, 3, 371-395

Gorard, S., See, BH and Siddiqui, N. (2017) *The trials of evidence-based education*, London: Routledge

Gorard, S., Siddiqui, N. and See, BH (2016a) An evaluation of Fresh Start as a catch-up intervention: And whether teachers can conduct trials, *Educational Studies*, 42, 1, 98-113

Gordon, J., Andrews, J. , Lichtenstein, E., Severson, H. and Akers, L. (2005) Disseminating a smokeless tobacco cessation intervention model to dental hygienists: A randomized comparison of personalized instruction and self-study methods, *Health Psychology, 24*, 5, 447-455

Gov.UK (2017) *Strategic School Improvement Fund*, https://www.gov.uk/guidance/strategic-school-improvement-fund

Graham, I. and Tetroe, J. (2009) Getting evidence into policy and practice: perspective of a health research funder, *Journal of the Canadian Academy of Child and Adolescent Psychiatry, 18*, 1, 46

Graham, I., Kothari, A. and McCutcheon, C. (2018) Moving knowledge into action for more effective practice, programmes and policy, *Implementation Science*, 13, doi:10.1186/s13012-017-0700-y

Graves, S. and Moore, A. (2018) How do you know what works, works for you? An investigation into the attitudes of senior leaders to using research evidence to inform teaching and learning in schools, *School Leadership and Management*, 38, 3, 259-277

Green, C., Taylor, C., Buckley, S. and Hean, S. (2016) Beyond synthesis: Augmenting systematic review procedures with practical principles to optimise impact and uptake in Educational Policy and Practice, *International Journal of Research and Method in Education*, 39, 3, 329-344

Green, L. (2008) Making research relevant: if it is an evidence-based practice, where's the practice-based evidence?, *Family Practice, 25*, suppl_1, i20-i24

Greenhalgh, T. and Wieringa, S. (2011) Is it time to drop the 'knowledge translation'metaphor? A critical literature review, *Journal of the Royal Society of Medicine, 104*, 12, 501-509

Griggs, J., Speight, S. and Javiera, C. (2016) *Ashford Teaching Alliance Research Champion: Evaluation report and executive summary*, London: Education Endowment Foundation

Grol, R. (2001) Successes and failures in the implementation of evidence-based guidelines for clinical practice, *Medical Care*, 39, 8 Suppl 2, 1146-1154

Grol, R. and Grimshaw, J. (1999) Evidence-based implementation of evidence-based medicine, *The Joint Commission Journal on Quality Improvement*, 25, 10, 503-513

Grol, R. and Grimshaw, J. (2003) From best evidence to best practice: effective implementation of change in patients' care, *The Lancet*, 326, 9391, 1225-1230

Grol, R. and Wensing, M. (2004) What drives change? Barriers to and incentives for achieving evidence-based practice, *Medical Journal of Australia*, *180*, 6 Suppl, S57

Gross, B., Jochim, A., Conaway, C., Schwartz, N., Keesler, V., Dempsey, K., Howley, C. and Kohler, P. (2015) The SEA of the Future: Building agency capacity for evidence-based policymaking, Volume 5, *https://www.crpe.org/publications/sea-future-building-agency-capacity-evidence-based-policymaking*

Gülmezoglu, A., Langer, A., Piaggio, G., Lumbiganon, P., Villar, J. and Grimshaw, J. (2007) Cluster randomized trial of an active, multifaceted information dissemination intervention based on The WHO Reproductive health library to change obstetric practices, *BJOG*, 114, 1, 16-23

Haines, A. Kuruvilla, S. and Borchert, M. (2004) Bridging the implementation gap between knowledge and action for health, *Bulletin of the World Health Organization*, 82(10)

Hammersley-Fletcher, L., Lewin, C., Davies, C., Duggan, J., Rowley, H. and Spink, E. (2015) *Evidence-based teaching: advancing capability and capacity for enquiry in schools: interim report,* Nottingham: National College for Teaching and Leadership

Hammond, A. and Klompenhouwer, P. (2005) Getting evidence into practice: implementing a behavioural joint protection education programme for people with rheumatoid arthritis, *British Journal of Occupational Therapy*, *68*, 1, 25-33

Harper, H. (2004) *The role of research in policy development : school sex education policy in Scotland since devolution,* (Electronic Thesis or Dissertation),

http://search.ebscohost.com/login.aspx?direct=true&db
=ddu&AN=B073948971608C95&site=ehost-live
Available from EBSCOhost ddu database.

Harvey, G. and Kitson, A. (2015) Translating evidence into healthcare policy and practice: single versus multi-faceted implementation strategies–is there a simple answer to a complex question?, *International Journal of Health Policy and Management*, 4, 3, 123

Harvey, G., Loftus-Hills, A., Rycroft-Malone, J., Titchen, A., Kitson, A., McCormack, B. and Seers, K. (2002) Getting evidence into practice: the role and function of facilitation, *Journal of Advanced Nursing*, 37, 6, 577-588

Hauck, S., Winsett, R. and Kuric, J. (2013) Leadership facilitation strategies to establish evidence-based practice in an acute care hospital, *Journal of Advanced Nursing*, 69, 3, 664-674

Hawkes, S., Aulakh, B., Jadeia, N., Jimenez, M., Buse, K., Anwar, I., Barge, S., Odubanjo, M., Shukla, A., Ghaffer. A. and Whitworth, J. (2016) Strengthening capacity to apply health research evidence in policy making: experience from four countries, *Health Policy and Planning*, 31, 2, 161-170

Haynes, A., Rowbotham, S., Redman, S., Brennan, S., Williamson, A. and Moore, G. (2018) What can we learn from interventions that aim to increase policy-makers' capacity to use research? A realist scoping review, *Health Research Policy and Systems*, 16, 31

Haynes, B. and Haines, A. (1998) Barriers and bridges to evidence based clinical practice, *BMJ*, 317, 7153, 273-276

Hazell, W. (2019) Education research 'has a problem and must get its house in order', *TES*, 5/2/19, https://www.tes.com/news/exclusive-education-research-has-problem-and-must-get-its-house-order

Head, B. (2015) Toward More "Evidence-Informed" Policy Making?, *Public Administration Review*, 76, 3, 472–484

Hemsley-Brown, J. and Sharp, C. (2003) The use of research to improve professional practice: A systematic review of the literature, *Oxford Review of Education, 29*, 4, 449-471

Hess, F. and Little, B. (2015) "Moneyball" for education, American Enterprise Institute

Hillage, J., Pearson, R., Anderson, A., Tamkin, P. (1998) *Excellence on research in schools*, Sudbury: DfEE

Hoeijmakers, M., Harting, J. and Jansen, M. (2013) Academic Collaborative Centre Limburg: a platform for knowledge transfer and exchange in public health policy, research and practice? *Health Policy*, 111, 2, 175-183

Honig, M. and Coburn, C. (2008) Evidence-based decision making in School District Central Offices: Toward a policy and research agenda, *Educational Policy*, 22, 4, 578-608

Honig, M., Venkateswaran, N. and McNeil, P. (2017) Research use as learning, *American Educational Research Journal*, 54, 5, 936-971

Humes, W., and Bryce, T. (2001) Scholarship, research and the evidential basis of policy development in education, *British Journal of Educational Studies*, 49, 3, 329-352

Husen, T. (1987) Policy impact of IEA research, *Comparative Education Review*, 31, 1

Ilic D. and Maloney S. (2014) Methods of teaching medical trainees evidence-based medicine: a systematic review, *Medical Education*, 48, 2, 124-135

Imani-Nasab, M., Seyedin, H., Yazdizadeh, B. and Majdzadeh, R. (2017) A qualitative assessment of the evidence utilisation for health policymaking on the basis of SUPPORT Tools in a developing country, *International Journal of Health Policy and Management*, 6, 8, 457-465

Innvær, S., Trommald, M. and Oxman, A. (2002) Health policy-makers' perceptions of their use of evidence: a systematic review, *Journal of Health Services Research and Policy*, 7, 4, 239-244

Jack, S., Dobbins, M., Tonmyr, L., Dudding, P., Brooks, S. and Kennedy, B. (2010) Research evidence utilization in policy development by child welfare administrators, *Child Welfare*, 89, 4, 83-100

Jackson E., Purnawati E., Shaxson L. (2018) How and when do policymakers use evidence? Taking politics into account, in Pellini A., Prasetiamartati B., Nugroho K., Jackson E., Carden F. (eds) *Knowledge, Politics and Policymaking in Indonesia*, Springer: Singapore

Jackson-Elmoore, C. (2005) Informing state policymakers: Opportunities for social workers, *Social Work*, 50, 3, 251-261

Jewell, C. and Bero L. (2008) "Developing good taste in evidence": Facilitators of and hindrances to evidence-informed health policymaking in state government, *The Milbank Quarterly*, 86, 2, 177-208

Jones, G. (2018) Where's the evidence for evidence-based practice improving pupil outcomes?, https://www.garyrjones.com/blog/

Jordan, E. and Coooper, P. (2016) *Building bridges*, Child Trends, Research Brief 2, https://www.childtrends.org/wp-content/uploads/2016/10/2016-56.1BuildingBridgesSharingWithPolicymakers.pdf

Kansagra, S. and Farley, T. (2012) Translating research into evidence-based practice, *American Journal of Public Health*, 102, 8, Letters

Kirigia, J., Pannenborg, C., Amore, L., Ghannem, H., IJsselmuiden, C. and Nabyonga_Orem, J. (2016) Global Forum 2015 dialogue on "From evidence to policy - thinking outside the box": perspectives to improve evidence uptake and good practices in the African Region, *BMC Health Services Research*, 16 (Suppl 4:215)

Kitson, A., Harvey, G. and McCormack, B. (1998) Enabling the implementation of evidence based practice: a conceptual framework, *BMJ Quality & Safety*, 7, 3, 149-158

Kitson, A., Rycroft-Malone, J., Harvey, G., McCormack, B., Seers, K. and Titchen, A. (2008) Evaluating the successful implementation of evidence into practice using the PARiHS framework: theoretical and practical challenges, *Implementation science, 3*, 1, 1

Koh, H., Oppenheimer, S., Massin-Short, S., Emmons, K., Geller, A. and Viswanath, K. (2010) Translating research evidence into practice to reduce health disparities: a social determinants approach, *American Journal of Public Health, 100*, S1, S72-S80

Korn, L., Betsch, C., Böhm, R. and Meier, N. (2018) Social nudging: The effect of social feedback interventions on vaccine uptake, *Health Psychology, 37*, 11, 1045-1054

Kothari, A., Birch, S. and Charles, C. (2005) "Interaction" and research utilisation in health policies and programs: does it work? *Health Policy, 71*, 1, 117-25

Lancaster, K. (2016) *Problematising the 'evidence-based' drug policy paradigm* (Thesis; PhD Doctorate), http://search.ebscohost.com/login.aspx?direct=true&db -ddu&AN-2A65EAED2F8DF4CD&site=ehost-live Available from EBSCOhost ddu database.

Langer, L., Tripney, J. and Gough, D. (2016) *The science of using science: Researching the use of research evidence in decision-making*, London: EPPI-Centre, UCL Institute of Education

Langlois, E., Montekio, V., Young, T., Song, K., Alcalde-Rabanal, J. and Tran, N. (2016) Enhancing evidence informed policymaking in complex health systems: lessons from multi-site collaborative approaches, *Health Research Policy and Systems, 14*, 20

LaRocca, R., Yost, J., Dobbins, M., Ciliska, D. and Butt, M. (2012) The effectiveness of knowledge translation strategies used in public health: a systematic review, *BMC Public Health, 12*, 751

Lassnigg, L. (2012) "Use of current best evidence": Promises and illusions, limitations and contradictions in the triangle of research, policy and practice, *International Journal of Training Research, 10*, 3, 179-203

Lavis, J., McLeod, C. and Gildiner, A. (2003) Measuring the impact of health research, *Journal of Health Services Research & Policy, 8*, 3, 165-170

Lawrence, R. (1990) Diffusion of the US Preventive Services Task Force recommendations into practice, *Journal of General Internal Medicine*, 5, 2, S99-S103

Lawton, R. (2014) Environmental science, economics, and policy: a context-sensitive approach to understanding the use of evidence in policy-making (Electronic Thesis or Dissertation), http://search.ebscohost.com/login.aspx?direct=true&db=ddu&AN=B6197947FFDD7E2A&site=ehost-live Available from EBSCOhost ddu database

Lawton, R. and Rudd, M. (2014) A narrative policy approach to environmental conservation, *Ambio*, 43, 7, 849-857

Levin, B., Cooper, A., Arjomand, S. and Thompson, K. (2011) Research use and its impact in secondary schools (978-1-896660-50-9), http://search.ebscohost.com/login.aspx?direct=true&db=eric&AN=ED535436&site=ehost-live

Lewis, E., Mayer, J., Slymen, D., Belch, G., Engelberg, M., Walker, K., . . . Elder, J. (2005) Disseminating a sun safety program to zoological parks: The effects of tailoring, *Health Psychology, 24*, 5, 456-462

Li, W. and Kamargianni, M. (2018) Providing quantified evidence to policy makers for promoting bike-sharing in heavily air-polluted cities: A mode choice model and policy simulation for Taiyuan-China, *Transportation Part A*, 111, 277-291

Lingard, B. (2013) The Impact of research on education policy in an era of evidence-based policy, *Critical Studies in Education*, 54, 2, 113-131

Lohr, K., Eleazer, K. and Mauskopf, J. (1998) Health policy issues and applications for evidence-based medicine and clinical practice guidelines, *Health Policy*, 46, 1, 1-19

Longjohn, M. (2012) Translating research into evidence-based practice, *American Journal of Public Health*, Letters, 102, 8

Lubienski, C., Scott, J. and DeBray, E. (2014) The politics of research production, promotion, and utilization in educational policy, *Educational Policy*, 28, pp.131-144

Macaulay, A. and Nutting, P. (2006) Moving the frontiers forward: incorporating community-based participatory research into practice-based research networks, *The Annals of Family Medicine*, *4*, 1, 4-7

MacIntyre, S., Chalmers, I., Horton, R. and Smith, R. (2001) Using evidence to inform health policy: Case study, *BMJ*, 322, 7280, 222-225

Mackie, T., Sheldrick, R., Hyde, J. and Leslie, L. (2015) Exploring the integration of systems and social sciences to study evidence use among child welfare policy-makers, *Child Welfare*, 94, 3, 33-58

Mady, C. (2013) Reducing the gap between educational research and second language teachers' knowledge, *Evidence & Policy: A Journal of Research, Debate and Practice*, 9, 2, 185-206

Mahoney, S. (2013) *Educational Research in the United States: A Survey of Pre-K-12 Teachers' Perceptions Regarding the Purpose, Conceptions, Use, Impact, and Dissemination* (Doctoral dissertation, Arizona State University)

Malin, J. and Lubienski, C. (2015) Educational expertise, advocacy, and media influence, *Education Policy Analysis Archives*, 23, 6

Mallidou, A., Atherton, P., Chan, L., Frisch, N., Glegg, S. and Scarrow, G. (2017) Protocol of a scoping review on knowledge translation competencies, *Systems Reviews*, 6, 93

Marquez, C., Johnson, A. , Jassemi, S., Park, J., Moore, J., Blaine, C., . . . Straus, S. (2018) Enhancing the uptake of systematic reviews of uptake of effects: What is the best format for health care managers and policymakers?, *Implementation Science*, 13, 84

Marston, G. and Watts, R. (2003) Tampering with the evidence: a critical appraisal of evidence-based policy-making, *The Drawing Board: an Australian Review of Public Affairs.*, 3, 3, 143-163

Maynard, B. and Dell, N. (2018) Use and impacts of Campbell systematic reviews on policy, practice, and research, *Research on Social Work Practice*, 28, 1, 13-18

McCluskey, A. and Cusick, A. (2002) Strategies for introducing evidence-based practice and changing clinician behaviour: A manager's toolbox, *Australian Occupational Therapy Journal*, *49*, 2, 63-70

McCormack, B., Kitson, A., Harvey, G., Rycroft-Malone, J., Titchen, A. and Seers, K. (2002) Getting evidence into practice: the meaning of context, *Journal of Advanced Nursing*, *38*, 1, 94-104

McLaughlin, H., Watts, C. and Beard, M. (2000) Just because it's happening doesn't mean it's working: using action research to improve practice in middle schools, *Phi Delta Kappan*, 82, 4, 284-290

McLean, R., Graham, D., Tetroe, J. and Volmink, J. (2018) Translating research into action: an international study of the role of research funders, *Health Research Policy and Systems*, 16(44)

McWilliam, C. (1997) Using a participatory research process to make a difference in policy on aging, *Canadian Public Policy /Analyse de Politiques*, 23, 70-89

Melnyk, B. (2007) The evidence-based practice mentor: A promising strategy for implementing and sustaining EBP in healthcare systems, *Worldviews on Evidence-Based Nursing*, *4*, 3, 123-125

Melnyk, B., Fineout-Overholt, E., Feinstein, N., Sadler, L. and Green-Hernandez, C. (2008) Nurse practitioner educators' perceived knowledge, beliefs, and teaching strategies regarding evidence-based practice: implications for accelerating the integration of evidence-based practice into graduate programs, *Journal of Professional Nursing*, *24*, 1, 7-13

Mendel, P., Meredith, L., Schoenbaum, M., Sherbourne, C., and Wells, K. (2008) Interventions in organizational and community context: a framework for building evidence on dissemination and implementation in health services research, *Administration and Policy in Mental Health and Mental Health Services Research*, 35, 1-2, 21-37

Menon, A., Korner-Bitensky, N., Kastner, M., McKibbon, K. and Straus, S. (2009) Strategies for rehabilitation professionals to move evidence-based knowledge into practice: a systematic review, *Journal of Rehabilitation Medicine*, 41, 13, 1024-1032

Miller, D. (1999) The black hole of education research, *Chronicle of Higher Education*, 45, 48, 17-18

Miller, W., Sorensen, J., Selzer, J. and Brigham, G. (2006) Disseminating evidence-based practices in substance abuse treatment: A review with suggestions, *Journal of Substance Abuse Treatment*, *31*, 1, 25-39

Milne, B., Lay-Yee, R., McLay, J., Tobias, M., Tuohy, P., Armstrong, A., . . . Davis, P. (2014) A collaborative approach to bridging the research-policy gap through the development of policy advice software, *Evidence & Policy*, 10, 1, 127-136

Mitton, C. Cave, E., McKenzie, E., Patten S. and Perry, B. (2007) Knowledge transfer and exchange: Review and synthesis of the literature, *The Milbank Quarterly*, 85(, 4, 729-768

Mold, J. and Peterson, K. (2005) Primary care practice-based research networks: working at the interface between research and quality improvement, *The Annals of Family Medicine*, 3, (suppl 1), S12-S20

Moore G., Redman S., Haines M. and Todd A. (2011) What works to increase the use of research in population health policy and programmes: a review, *Evidence and Policy*, 7, 3, 277–305

Mosteller, F. and Boruch, R. (2002) *Evidence matters: Randomized trials in education research*, Brookings Institution Press

Moulding, N., Silagy, C. and Weller, D. (1999) A framework for effective management of change in clinical practice: dissemination and implementation of clinical practice guidelines, *Quality in Health Care*, 8, 177–183

Murthy, L., Shepperd, S., Clarke, M., Garner, S., Lavis, J., Perrier, L., Roberts, N. and Straus, S. (2012) Interventions to improve the use of systematic reviews in decision-making by health systems managers, policy makers and clinicians, *Cochrane Databases of Systematic Reviews*, Sept 12 (9).

National Research Council (1999) *Improving student learning:
a strategic plan for educational research and its
utilization*, Washington DC: National Academy Press

Naude, C., Zani, B., Ongolo-Zogo, P., Wiysonge, C., Dudley,
L., Kredo, T., . . . Young, T. (2015) Research evidence
and policy: Qualitative study in selected provinces in
South Africa and Cameroon, *Implementation Science*,
10, 126

Nelson, S., Leffler, J. and Hansen, B. (2009) Towards a
research agenda for understanding and improving the
use of research evidence,
http://search.ebscohost.com/login.aspx?direct=true&db
=eric&AN=ED506962&site=ehost-live

Newhouse, R. (2007) Creating infrastructure supportive of
evidence-based nursing practice: Leadership
strategies, *Worldviews on Evidence-Based Nursing*, 4,
1, 21-29

NFER (2017) *The Literacy Octopus*, EEF,
https://educationendowmentfoundation.org.uk/projects
-and-evaluation/projects/the-literacy-octopus-
communicating-and-engaging-with-research/

Nilsen, P. (2015) Making sense of implementation theories,
models and frameworks, *Implementation Science*, 10, 1,
53

Noyes, A. and Adkins, M. (2016) The Impact of Research on
Policy: A Case of Qualifications Reform, *British
Journal of Educational Studies*, 64:4, 449-465

Nutley, S., Davies, H. and Walter, I. (2002) *Evidence based
policy and practice: Cross sector lessons from the UK*,
ESRC UK Centre for Evidence Based Policy and
Practice, Working Paper 9

Nutley, S., Walter, I. and Davies, H. (2003) From knowing to
doing: a framework for understanding the evidence-
into-practice agenda, *Evaluation*, 9, 2, 125-148

Nutley, S., Walter, I. and Davies, H. (2007) *Using research:
How research can inform public services*, Bristol: The
Policy Press

Oliver, K., Innvar, S., Lorenc, T., Woodman, J. and Thomas, J.
(2014) A systematic review of barriers to and facilitators

of the use of evidence by policymakers, *BMC Health Services Research*, 14, 2

Oman, K., Duran, C. and Fink, R. (2008) Evidence-based policy and procedures: an algorithm for success, *The Journal of Nursing Administration*, 38, 1, 47-51

Ongolo-Zogo, P., Lavis, J., Tomson, G. and Sewankambo, N. (2014) Initiatives supporting evidence informed health system policymaking in Cameroon and Uganda: a comparative historical case study, *BMC Health Services Research*, 14, 612

Orem, J., Mafigiri, D., Marchal, B., Ssengooba, F., Macq, J. and Criel, B. (2012) Research, evidence and policymaking: the perspectives of policy actors on improving uptake of evidence in health policy development and implementation in Uganda, *BMC Public Health*, 12, 109

Palmer, G. (2000) Evidence-based health policy-making, hospital funding and health insurance, *The Medical Journal Of Australia*, 172, 3, 130-133

Palmer, J. (1999) Research Matters: A call for the application of empirical evidence to the task of improving the quality and impact of environmental education, *Cambridge Journal of Education*, 29, 3, 379-395

Pappaioanou, M., Malison. M., Wilkins, K., Otto, B., Goodman, R., Churchill, R., White, M. and Thacker, S. (2003) Strengthening capacity in developing countries for evidence-based public health: the data for decision-making project, *Social Science and Medicine*, 57, 10, 1925-1937

Park, S. J. (2013) Do Highly Qualified Teachers Use More Effective Instructional Practices than other Teachers: The Mediating Effect of Instructional Practices, Society for Research on Educational Effectiveness Conference, 7th-9th March, Washington D.C. Available from http://files.eric.ed.gov/fulltext/ED563054.pdf [Accessed 28th June 2016].

Parkhurst, J. (2017) *The politics of evidence: From evidence-based policy to the good governance of evidence*, Abingdon, Oxon: Routledge

Pawson, R. (2006) *Evidence-Based Policy: A Realist Perspective*, London: Sage

Pederson, H., Halpin, D. and Rasmussen, A. (2015) Who gives evidence to Parliamentary Committees? A comparative investigation of Parliamentary Committees and their constituencies, *The Journal of Legislative Studies*, 21, 3, 408-427

Peirson, L., Ciliska, D., Dobbins, M. and Mowat, D. (2012) Building capacity for evidence informed decision making in public health: a case study of organizational change, *BMC Public Health*, 12, 1, 137

Penuel, W., Briggs, D., Davidson, K., Herlihy, C., Sherer, D., Hill, H., . . . Allen, A. (2017) How school and district leaders access and use research, AERA Open, https://journals.sagepub.com/doi/abs/10.1177/2332858 417705370

Perrier L., Mrklas K., Lavis J., Straus S. (2011) Interventions encouraging the use of systematic reviews by health policymakers and managers: a systematic review, *Implementation Science*, 6, 43

Perry, A., Amadeo, C., Fletcher, M. and Walker, E. (2010) Instinct or Reason: How education policy is made and how we might make it better, CfBT, https://www.educationdevelopmenttrust.com/~/media/ EDT/Reports/Research/2010/r-instinct-or-reason-2010.pdf

Peterson, M. (2018) In the shadow of politics, Journal of Health Politics Policy and Law, 43, 3, 341-376

Petkovic, J., Welch, V., Jacob, M., Yoganathan, M., Ayala, A., Cunningham, H. and Tugwell, P. (2010) *Do evidence summaries increase health policy-makers' use of evidence from systematic reviews?*, Campbell Collaboration, https://campbellcollaboration.org/library/evidence-summaries-for-policymakers.html

Pew Charitable Trusts (2014) *Evidence-based policymaking - A guide for effective government*, http://www.pewtrusts.org/~/media/assets/2014/11/-

evidencebasedpolicymakingaguideforeffectivegovernm
ent.pdf

Pogro, S. (2017) The failure of the US education research
establishment to identify effective practices: beware
effective practices policies, *Education Policy Analysis
Archives*, 25, 5

Powell A., Davies H., Nutley S. (2017) Facing the challenges
of research-informed knowledge mobilization:
'Practising what we preach?', Public Administration, 1–
17, https://doi.org/10.1111/padm.12365

Powell, D., Diamond, K., Burchinal, M. and Koehler, M.
(2010) Effects of an early literacy professional
development intervention on head start teachers and
children, *Journal of Educational Psychology*, 102, 2,
299

Procter, R. (2013) Teachers and research: What they value and
what they do, *Journal of Pedagogic Development*, 3, 1

Public Accounts Committee (2015) *Funding for disadvantaged
pupils*, HC 327, 9 October 2015,
https://publications.parliament.uk/pa/cm201516/cmsele
ct/cmpubacc/327/327.pdf

Reid, A. (2016) The use and abuse of research in the public
domain, *Australian Educational Researcher*, 43, 1, 75-
91

Rickinson, M., de Bruin, K., Walsh, L. and Hall, M. (2017)
What can evidence-use in practice learn from evidence-
use in policy? *Educational Research*, 59, 2, 173-189.
doi:10.1080/00131881.2017.1304306

Ritter, A. Hughes, C., Lancaster, K. and Hoppe, R. (2018)
Using the Advocacy Coalition Framework and Multiple
Streams policy theories to examine the role of evidence,
research and other types of knowledge in drug policy,
*Addiction*, 113, 8

Roberts, J. (2018) "I might as well be a robot", *TES*, 9/1/18,
https://www.tes.com/news/tes-magazine/tes-
magazine/i-might-well-be-a-robot

*Rohwer, A., Motaze, N., Rehfuess, E. and Young, T. (2017) E-
learning of evidence-based health care (EBHC) to
increase EBHC competencies in healthcare*

professionals: a systematic review, *Campbell Systematic Reviews, 4*, doi:*10.4073/csr.2017.4*

Rolle, I., Zaidi, I., Scharff, J., Jones, D., Firew, A., Enquselassie, F., Negash, A., Deyessa, N., Mitile, G., Sunderland, N. and Nsubuga, P. (2011) Leadership in strategic information (LSI) building skilled public health capacity in Ethiopia, *BMC Research Notes*, 4, 1, 292

Rose, J., Thomas, S., Zhang, L., Edwards, A., Augero, A. and Roney, P. (2017) *Research Learning Communities*, https://educationendowmentfoundation.org.uk/public/fi les/Projects/Evaluation_Reports/Research_Learning_C ommunities.pdf

Rosenbaum, S., Glenton, C. and Oxman, A. (2010) Summary-of-findings tables in Cochrane reviews improved understanding and rapid retrieval of key information, *Journal of Clinical Epidemiology*, 63, 6, 620-626

Rosenfield, S. and Berninger, V. (2009, Eds.) *Implementing Evidence-Based Academic Interventions in School Settings*, OUP

Rosenstock, L. and Lee, L. (2002) Attacks on science: the risks to evidence-based policy, *American Journal of Public Health*, 92, 1, 14-18

Royal Society/British Academy (2018) *Harnessing educational research*, https://royalsociety.org/~/media/policy/projects/rs-ba-educational-research/educational-research-report.pdf

Ruangkanchanasetr, S. (1993) Laboratory investigation utilization in pediatric out-patient department Ramathibodi Hospital, *J Med Assoc Thai*, 76, Suppl 2, 194-208

Rubenstein, L. and Pugh, J. (2006) Strategies for promoting organizational and practice change by advancing implementation research, *Journal of General Internal Medicine*, 21, 2, S58

Rutter, J. (2012) *Evidence and evaluation in policy-making: A problem of supply or demand?*, Institute for Government

Rycroft-Malone, J., Gill, H. and Kitson, A. (2002) Getting evidence into practice: ingredients for change, *Nursing Standard (through 2013)*, 16, 37, 38

Schilling, J., Giles-Corti, B. and Sallis, J. (2009) Connecting active living research and public policy, *Journal of Public Health Policy*, 30, S1-S15

Schmittdiel, J., Grumbach, K. and Selby, J. (2010) System-based participatory research in health care: an approach for sustainable translational research and quality improvement, *The Annals of Family Medicine*, 8, 3, 256-259

See, BH (2017) Evaluating the evidence in evidence-based policy and practice, *Research in Education*, http://journals.sagepub.com/doi/abs/10.1177/00345237 17741915

See, BH, Gorard, S. and Siddiqui, N. (2016) Can teachers use research evidence in practice?: A pilot study of the use of feedback to enhance learning, *Educational Research*, 58, 1, 56-72

Seers, K., Crichton, N., Carroll, D., Richards, S. and Saunders, T. (2004) Evidence-based postoperative pain management in nursing: is a randomized-controlled trial the most appropriate design?, *Journal of Nursing Management*, 12, 3, 183-193

Sen, G., Virani, A. and Iyer, A. (2017) *Translating health research to policy: breaking through impermeability barrier*, http://www.theimpactinitiative.net/impact-lab/collection/translating-health-research-policy

Shroff, Z., Aulakh, B., Gilson, L., Agyepong, I. A., Fadi El, J. and Ghaffar, A. (2015) Incorporating research evidence into decision-making processes: researcher and decision-maker perceptions from five low- and middle-income countries, *Health Research Policy and Systems*, 13, 70

Siddiqi, K., Newell, J. and Robinson, M. (2005) Getting evidence into practice: what works in developing countries?, *International Journal for Quality in Health Care*, 17, 5, 447-454

Siddiqui, N., Gorard, S. and See, BH (2015) Accelerated Reader as a literacy catch-up intervention during the primary to secondary school transition phase, *Educational Review*, 68, 2, 139-154

Simons, M., Zurynski, Y., Cullis, J., Morgan, M. and Davidson, A. (2018) *Does evidence-based medicine training improve doctors' knowledge, practice and patient outcomes? A systematic review of the evidence, Medical Teacher*, 1-7

Simpson, A. (2017) The misdirection of public policy: comparing and combining standardised effect sizes, *Journal of Education Policy*, 32, 4, 450-466

Simpson, R. (2003) Policy-related research issues and perspectives, *Focus on Autism*, 18, 3, 192-196

Sin, C. (2008) The role of intermediaries in getting evidence into policy and practice: some useful lessons from examining consultancy–client relationships, *Evidence & Policy: A Journal of Research, Debate and Practice*, 4, 1, 85-103

Sirat, M. and Azman, N. (2014) Malaysia's National Higher Education Research Institute (IPPTN): narrowing the research-policy gap in a dynamic higher education system, *Studies in Higher Education*, 39, 8, 1451-1462

Sisk (1993) Improving the Use of Research-Based Evidence in Policy Making: Effective Care in Pregnancy and Childbirth in the United States, *The Milbank Quarterly*, 71, 3, 477-496

Slavin, R. (2017) *Education policy in the age of proven school and classroom approaches*, https://www.huffingtonpost.com/robert-e-slavin/education-policy-in-the-a_b_13513714.html

Slavin, R., Cheung, A., Homes, G., Madden, N. and Chamberlain A. (2013) Effects of a Data-Driven District Reform Model on State Assessments, *AERJ*, 50, 2

Smith, A. (2003) Scientifically based research and evidence-based education: A Federal Policy context, *Research and Practice for Persons with Severe Disabilities*, 28, 3, 126-132

Smith, W. (2000) Evidence for the effectiveness of techniques to change physician behaviour, *Chest*, 118, 2, 8S-17S

Sparks, S. (2018) Teachers want education research, *Education Week*, 27th November, http://blogs.edweek.org/edweek/inside-school-research/2018/11/get_teachers_research_on_education.html?cmp=RSS-FEED

Speight, S., Callahan, M., Griggs, J. and Javiera, C. (2016) *Rochdale research into practice: evaluation report and executive summary*, London: Education Endowment Foundation

Strambler, M. and McKown, C. (2013) Promoting student engagement through evidence-based action research with teachers, *Journal of Educational and Psychological Consultation*, 23, 2, 87-114

Sussman, S., Valente, T., Rohrbach, L., Skara, S. and Ann Pentz, M. (2006) Translation in the health professions: converting science into action, *Evaluation and the Health Professions*, 29, 1, 7-32

Swinburn, B., Gill, T. and Kumanyika, S. (2005) Obesity prevention: a proposed framework for translating evidence into action, *Obesity Reviews*, 6, 1, 23-33

Tabak, R., Khoong, E., Chambers, D. and Brownson, R. (2012) Bridging research and practice: models for dissemination and implementation research, *American Journal of Preventive Medicine*, 43, 3, 337-350

Tapp, H. and Dulin, M. (2010) The science of primary health-care improvement: potential and use of community-based participatory research by practice-based research networks for translation of research into practice, *Experimental Biology and Medicine*, 235, 3, 290-299

Taylor, C. and Gorard, S. (2002) *The RBCN Consultation exercise: Stakeholder Report*, Occasional Paper 50, Cardiff University School of Social Sciences

Taylor, R., Reeves, B., Ewings, P. and Taylor, R. (2004) Critical appraisal skills training for health care professionals: a randomized controlled trial, *BMC Medical Education*, 4, 30–40

The Guardian (2017) David Laws: "the quality of education policy-making is poor", *The Guardian*, 1/8/17, https://www.theguardian.com/education/2017/aug/01/d avid-laws-education-policy-schools-minister-thinktank-epi

Thomas I., Mackie R., Sheldrick, C., Hyde, J. and Leslie, L. (2015) Exploring the Integration of Systems and Social Sciences to Study Evidence Use among Child Welfare Policy-makers, *Child Welfare*, 94, 3, 33-58

Thompson D., Estabrooks C., Scott-Findlay S., Moore K. and Wallin L. (2007) Interventions aimed at increasing research use in nursing: a systematic review, *Implementation Science*, 2, 15

Thomson, P., Angus, N. and Scott, J. (2000) Building a framework for getting evidence into critical care education and practice, *Intensive and Critical Care Nursing*, 16, 3, 164-174

Tranmer J., Lochaus-Gerlach J., Lam M. (2002) The effect of staff nurse participation in a clinical nursing research project on attitude towards, access to, support of and use of research in acute care settings, *Canadian Journal of Nurse Leadership*, 15, 18-26

Traynor, R., DeCorby, K. and Dobbins, M. (2014) Knowledge brokering in public health: a tale of two studies, *Public Health*, 128, 6, 533-544

Tricco, A., Wasifa, Z., Rios, P., Nincic, V., Khan, P., Ghassemi, M., . . . Langlois, E. (2018) Engaging policy makers, health system managers and policy analysts in the knowledge synthesis process, *Implementation Science*, 13, 31

Uneke, C., Ezeoha, A., Ndukwe, C., Oyibo, P. and Onwe, F. (2012) Promotion of evidence-informed health policymaking in Nigeria: bridging the gap between researchers and policymakers, *Global Public Health*, 7, 7, 750-765

Uneke, C., Ezeoha, A., Uro-Chukwu, H., Ezeonu, C. and Igboji, J. (2018) Promoting researchers and policy-makers collaboration in evidence-informed policymaking in Nigeria, *International Journal of Health Policy Management*, 7, 6, 522-531

Uneke, C., Ezeoha, A., Uro-Chukwu, H., Ezeonu, C., Ogbu, O., Onwe, F., Edoga, C. (2015a) Enhancing the capacity of policy-makers to develop evidence-informed policy brief on infectious diseases of poverty in Nigeria, *International Journal of Health Policy and Management*, 4, 9, 599-610

Uneke, C., Ndukwe, C., Ezeoha, A., Uro-Chukwu, H., Ezeonu, C. (2015b) Implementation of a health policy advisory committee as a knowledge translation platform: the Nigeria experience, *International Journal of Health Policy Management*, 4, 3, 161–168

University of Bristol (2017) Research Learning Communities, https://educationendowmentfoundation.org.uk/projects -and-evaluation/projects/research-learning-communities/

Urwick, J. (2014) Who will listen to educational researchers? Reflections on the research–policy relationship in the global South, with illustrations from Africa, *Compare*, 44, 4, 545-565

Valentine, A., DeAngelo, D., Alegría, M. and Cook, B. (2014) Translating disparities research to policy: A qualitative study of state mental health policymakers' perceptions of mental health care disparities report cards, *Psychological Services*, 11, 4, 377-387

van de Arend, J. (2016) *Connecting research and policy: how linkages support the use of research evidence in social policymaking*, (PhD), The University of Queensland, https://espace.library.uq.edu.au/data/UQ_411282/s425 26993_final_thesis.pdf?Expires=1531784801&Signatu re=d3zjHuBD~1W2hSz6R2jynWTHAsKWXjNTykQj q0Qaj3zzY2zhF991xLSx6naRAEGQNameW50q~- tWb-pmZQVIY2JR6hAQH9LCLT- PlbOq5R8dUO6HUQWznRkoeqrtgALhV9pFxFKArg pVh9BCWoFhPQEyP5aUaOcb6gIm5qTUBFOgrwXe BfPumlVF4Y7OgH4Ig8HnEN~KUCmPTUCpurAmpj koA5clJJ~IVqK2VFv-tM- Gm4lt76JUNcWGAkEHCPiq9UzJs-

eyWeKCxWvnw09XlcIp5XFtJKLZIv6NpmVsaZBsPo
rxHIHt61mXXnUkOJHNT7i7s9KG6eCzqPlLQZ07Ug
__&Key-Pair-Id=APKAJKNBJ4MJBJNC6NLQ

van de Goor, I., Hamalainen, R., Syed, A., Lau, C., Sandu, P., Spitters, H., . . . and Aro, A. R. (2017) Determinants of evidence use in public health policymaking: results from a study across six EU countries, *Health Policy*, 121, 3, 273-281

Vujcich, D. (2016) Where there is no evidence, and where evidence is not enough: an analysis of policy-making to reduce the prevalence of Australian indigenous smoking, *Frontiers in Public Health*, 4, 228

Wandersman, A., Duffy, J., Flaspohler, P., Noonan, R., Lubell, K., Stillman, L., ... and Saul, J. (2008) Bridging the gap between prevention research and practice: The interactive systems framework for dissemination and implementation, *American Journal of Community Psychology*, 41, 3-4, 171-181

Waqa, G., Mavoa, H., Snowdon, W., Moodie, M., Schultz, J., McCabe, M., Kremer, P. and Swinburn, B. (2013) Knowledge brokering between researchers and policymakers in Fiji to develop policies to reduce obesity: a process evaluation, *Implementation Science*, 8, 1, 74

Ward, V., House, A. and Hamer, S. (2009a) Developing a framework for transferring knowledge into action: a thematic analysis of the literature, *Journal of Health Services Research and Policy*, 14, 3, 156-164.

Ward, V., House, A. and Hamer, S. (2009b) Knowledge brokering: exploring the process of transferring knowledge into action, *BMC Health Services Research*, 9, 1, 12

Ward, V., House, A. and Hamer, S. (2009c) Knowledge brokering: the missing link in the evidence to action chain?, *Evidence and Policy*, 5, 3, 267-279

Wentworth, L., Mazzeo, C. and Connolly, F. (2017) Research practice partnerships: A strategy for promoting evidence-based decision-making in education, *Educational Research*, 59, 2, 241-255

Whitty, G. (2016) *Research and policy in education: Evidence, ideology and impact*, Trentham Books

Williams, A. (2010) Is Evidence-Based Policy Making Really Possible?, in Colebatch, H., Hoppe, R. and Noordegraaf, M. (Eds.) *Working for Policy* (pp. 195-210), Amsterdam: Amsterdam University Press

Williams, M. (2016) *To what extent has research been used to inform anti-poverty policy in Ghana*, (Electronic Thesis or Dissertation), http://search.ebscohost.com/login.aspx?direct=true&db =ddu&AN=A2CB93E394CC211B&site=ehost-live Available from EBSCOhost ddu database

Wilson, J., Armoutliev, E., Yakunina, E. and Werth, J. (2009) Practicing psychologists' reflections on evidence-based practice in psychology, *Professional Psychology: Research and Practice*, 40, 4, 403-409

Winters, C., and Echeverri, R. (2012) Teaching strategies to support evidence-based practice, *Critical Care Nurse*, *32*, 3, 49-54

Witting, A. (2017) Insights from 'policy learning' on how to enhance the use of evidence by policymakers, *Palgrave Communications*, 3, 49

Wolgemuth, J., Hicks, T. and Agosto, V. (2017) Unpacking assumptions in research synthesis, *Educational Researcher*, 46, 3, 131-139

Wyatt, J., Paterson-Brown, S., Johanson, R., Altman, D., Bradburn, M. and Fisk, N. (1998) Randomised Trial of educational visits to enhance use of systematic reviews in 25 obstetric units, *BMJ*, 317, 7165, 1041-1046

Yost J., Ganann R., Thompson D., Aloweni F., Newman K., Hazzan A., McKibbon A., Dobbins M. and Ciliska D. (2015) The effectiveness of knowledge translation interventions for promoting be shownevidence-informed decision-making among nurses in tertiary care: a systematic review and meta-analysis, *Implementation Science*, 10, 1, 1-15

Zardo, P. and Collie, A. (2015) Type, frequency and purpose of information used to inform public health policy and program decision-making, *BMC Public Health*, 15, 381

Zardo, P., Barnett, A., Suzor, N. and Cahill, T. (2018) Does engagement predict research use? An analysis of The Conversation annual survey 2016, *Plos One*, doi:https://doi.org/10.1371/journal.pone.0192290

Zhao, Y. (2017) What works may hurt: Side effects in education, *Journal of Educational Change*, 18, 1, 1–19

Zimmermann, K. (2004) Advising policymakers through the media, *The Journal of Economic Education*, 35, 4, 395-406

Zlotnik, J. (2007) Evidence-based practice and social work education: A view from Washington, *Research on Social Work Practice*, 17, 5, 625-629

Printed in Poland
by Amazon Fulfillment
Poland Sp. z o.o., Wrocław